MONARCH

ILLUSTRATED GUIDE TO EMBROIDERY

INTRODUCTION BY
PAM DAWSON

MONARCH PRESS · NEW YORK

© Marshall Cavendish Limited 1972, 1973, 1974, 1975, 1976, 1977

This volume first published 1977
Reprinted 1977

Standard Book Number: 0-671-18770-8

Library of Congress Catalog Card Number: 76-29159

Published by
MONARCH PRESS, a Simon & Schuster Division of
Gulf & Western Corporation
Simon & Schuster Building
1230 Avenue of the Americas
New York, N.Y. 10020

Printed in Great Britain

Picture Credits:
American Museum in Britain 3
Beta Pictures 30
Camera Press 5, 8, 9, 23, 27, 36, 116
Cooper Bridgeman 11
100 Idees de Marie Claire 12
PAF International 14, 15, 16
Transworld 29

Photographers: Steve Bicknell, John Carter, Alan Duns, Melvin Grey,
Peter Heinz, Tony Horth, Jeany, Peter Kibbles, Chris Lewis, Sandra Lousada,
Dick Millar, Julian Nieman, Kjell Nilsson, Roger Phillips, Peter Pugh Cook,
Iain Reid, John Ryan, Jill Smyth, Jean Claude Volpeliere, Paul Williams.

CONTENTS

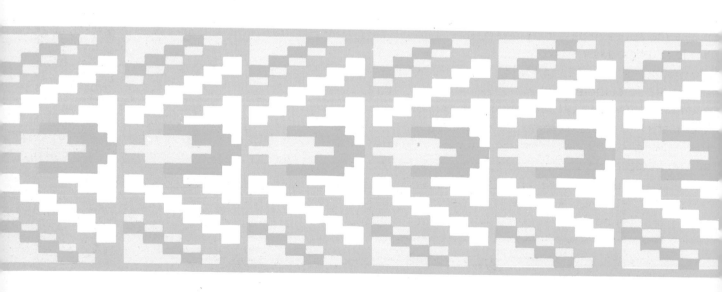

AN INTRODUCTION TO EMBROIDERY

Anyone who has an interest in needle crafts has a special love for the beautiful art of embroidery. The structure of many different types of fabric, whether bought or hand-made, can be greatly enhanced by this age-old and ever more lovely form of embellishment. It is small wonder that the popularity of this craft has grown in the way that it has through the centuries. Today, actually more people are embroidering things than ever before, although love and appreciation for embroidered decoration have always existed in man, evidenced by the very early origin of the craft.

Even before primitive man had learned to cure skins or weave and knot fabrics, he had already begun the search for some outlet for his creative ability and some way of satisfying his love for beauty. Body painting was, and still is in some remote areas, a form of art which satisfied this very early need. Once he began to clothe himself, this creative urge extended itself to finding some form of decoration with which he could display his own individuality on the warm protective covering he had learned to make for himself.

The art of embroidering with a needle had already reached a high standard in Old Testament days and has since formed a part of the cultural development of almost every nation in the world. Embroidery has evolved into many different forms, and the overall names of some of these categories have a ring of grandeur about them. Groups of stitches which comprise Hardanger, Hedebo and Assisi techniques all evoke memories of past glory and history.

Some stitches, such as cross stitch and chain stitch are so simple that a child can easily master them, while others are so complex that even a small piece could eventually become a prized heirloom. In England, the Victorians had a passion for exquisite embroidery and their way of teaching as many stitches as possible to all who would learn was one that could well be adopted today. A child would be encouraged to begin a sampler of stitches which would be continued throughout his adult life thus forming a unique and lasting record of his achievement. Another popular form of sampler that many children worked was made entirely in cross stitch, depicting a series of pictures and quotations, mostly biblical, and proudly completed with a signature and date.

Many of the most popular stitches today are still very simple ones, for example, the lazy daisy and cross stitches, and French knots, smocking and backstitch. Simple needlepoint too and even some drawn thread work are relatively easy to do.

In this book we have attempted to offer clear and concise instructions, and simple illustrations of the working methods for the basic stitches, as well as for those which call for much more advanced techniques. Our instructions are very easy to follow and the text is presented in a logical way, allowing you to begin with something quite simple but effective, before progressing on to more difficult work. With the aid of this book we hope that you will extend your knowledge of the craft and explore the many possibilities of this beautiful, decorative art form.

Pam Dawson

1

BASIC SKILLS
EQUIPMENT

The basic tools for embroidery are simple: a pair of good embroidery scissors with fine points; a pair of paper-cutting scissors or blunt, older scissors for making a design of cut paper shapes – embroidery scissors should never be used to cut paper; a thimble; assorted needles, i.e. crewels, betweens, sharps, tapestry, a large chenille needle, or a thick one, such as is used in the joining of heavy knit garments, to take heavy threads through to the back of your work by means of a sling for certain embroidery stitches. The correct needle for particular project will be given in instructions.

Other essentials are beeswax for waxing thread necessary for some types of embroidery; a piece of tailor's chalk or a white dressmaking pencil for use on darker materials; basting thread; pins; embroidery threads; and a frame to hold the fabric firm as you work.

Embroidery fabrics

There are many fabrics suitable for embroidery, providing a constant source of inspiration for both beginner and expert. Linen is a favorite choice and is woven in many weights and colors and in both soft and coarser textures. Suitable cotton materials include such fabrics as poplin, organdy, gingham and glazed cotton. Woolen fabrics are suitable for many stitches, particularly even weave wools, flannels and wool tweeds, both in light and heavy weights. There is also silk in all its varying weights and textures, from thin Chinese silk to raw silk and the heavier silk tweeds. Many man-made home furnishing fabrics make the choice for the needleworker even wider since they serve as excellent backgrounds for stitchery.

A comprehensive reference chart, to help guide you in your choice of fabrics, threads and needles, is given later.

Embroidery hoops

To achieve a really professional finish in embroidery, a hoop is essential. It holds the fabric taut while you are working and helps you to form the stitches evenly and accurately as you go along.

Before starting work, overcast the edges of the fabric to prevent the edges from fraying once the fabric has been placed in the frame.

There are two main types of embroidery hoops – the round, or tambour, frame which is used for small pieces of work with surface or counted embroidery, and the traditional slate frame which is used for large pieces of embroidery.

Round hoops

These are available in different sizes from 3 inches to 12 inches diameter and are usually made from wood, although it is possible to buy aluminum ones which hold the fabric more securely.

A hoop consists of two circles which fit securely one inside the other. The fabric is stretched over the smaller one and the larger one slips on top of it and holds the fabric in place. This second hoop sometimes has a screw which can be adjusted to tighten or slacken the fabric as required. To prevent the fabric from slipping through the hoop when you are mounting it, you can bind the inner hoop with tape or strips of thin cotton fabric first. To mount the fabric, stretch the piece to be embroidered over the inner hoop, keeping the grain of the fabric square, press down the outer hoop and adjust the screw if necessary.

Square frames

Embroidery worked on a stretcher rarely needs pressing before mounting and this is a great advantage when various types of stitchery have been combined, each of which might react differently to heat or dampness.

The frames are available in different sizes from about 18 inches to 30 inches, although it is possible to obtain even larger ones, often combined with a floor stand.

The stretcher consists of two rollers which form the top and bottom of the rectangle and two flat strips which form the side slats of the frame. The side pieces have a series of holes down their length which enables them to be fitted into the rollers at any point with wooden pegs or screws to make a frame the right size for your em-

broidery. Each roller has a strip of tape or webbing nailed along the edge to which the fabric is firmly sewn.

For embroidery which will not be damaged by rolling, such as petit point and other forms of needlepoint, it is possible to buy frames with rotating rollers so the work can be rolled up as it progresses.

A less expensive substitute for the rectangular frame is a canvas painting stretcher, obtainable in various sizes from art suppliers. When this is used the embroidery fabric is attached to it with thumb tacks, care being taken to insure that enough thumb tacks are used and that the fabric is firmly pinned so that it is completely taut.

Preparing a stretcher

Preparing a frame for embroidery is known as dressing the frame.

1 Assemble the stretcher by inserting the side pieces into the rollers at the required height and securing them in place.

2 Mark the centers of the tape or webbing on both rollers with colored thread.

3 If the fabric is likely to fray turn down a $\frac{1}{2}$ inch hem along the top and bottom edges of the fabric and sew them in place. Mark the center points of the edges.

4 Turn under the side edges of the fabric $\frac{1}{2}$ inch around a piece of cord or string to give added strength for attaching it to the side slats. Sew very securely in place.

5 Match the center of the top edge of the fabric to the center of the roller and pin it

in position, working from the center out to each side. Then sew using strong thread.

6 Repeat on the bottom roller so that the fabric is quite taut between the two rollers.

7 To secure the fabric to the side pieces, use very strong thread or fine string and a heavy needle and lace them together using a diagonal stitch and placing the stitches about 1 inch apart. Leave a fairly

long piece of string at the ends, pull taut, then tie through the last hole at the top and bottom of the slat.

Attaching fine fabrics

If you are mounting a very fine fabric, such as silk or organdy which is likely to tear if it is laced, a different method of attaching the edges to the side slats should be used.

1 Using long pieces of $\frac{3}{4}$ inch wide blanket or bias tape, start at the top and pin the tape to the side edge of the fabric, placing the pin about $\frac{1}{2}$ inch from the edge.

2 Fold the tape back over the pin (to prevent it from pricking you while you work) and take it over and around the side slat. Pin it to the fabric about 1 inch further down, then take it over the side slat again. Continue in this way to the bottom of the fabric and then complete the opposite side in the same way.

Backing the fabric

If you are using a selection of threads of different weights or adding beads to the embroidery which might be too heavy for the fabric, it is advisable to back it for extra strength. The backing can be of washed linen, cotton or muslin – heavy canvas is normally too firmly woven for this purpose.

The embroidery is worked through the double thickness and when it is finished the surplus backing fabric is cut off and trimmed back to the line of embroidery. The method of dressing a frame when using a backing is slightly different.

1 Baste a line down the center of both the backing and the embroidery fabric. Working on a flat surface, place the fabric on the backing, matching the center lines. Pin in position, working out from the center and with the pins pointing inward to avoid puckering. Take care not to stretch either layer. Firmly baste the layers together around the entire outer edge.

2 Turn under the side edges of the backing for $\frac{1}{2}$ inch, enclosing a piece of cord or string to give strength for attaching it to the side slats. Sew very securely in place.

3 Attach the top and bottom edges to the rollers and lace the sides to the slats as for unbacked fabrics.

Backing small pieces of embroidery

If the embroidery fabric is much smaller than the backing fabric, pin it in position on the backing using fine pins or needles to avoid leaving marks. Sew over it by taking the needle from the embroidery fabric, and down into the backing fabric $\frac{3}{8}$ inch above the edge of the embroidery fabric. This pulls the fabric completely taut on the backing.

DESIGN TRANSFERS

There are three main methods of transferring embroidery designs to fabric and usually the type of design and fabric decides which is most suitable. Whichever method you do choose, however, it is normally best to transfer the design after the fabric has been mounted into a frame since it may become rubbed or obliterated if you transfer it before mounting.

For all methods, start by making a tracing of your design – whether it is freely drawn, copied from an illustration, or composed of cut paper shapes – using tracing paper and a non-smudge pencil.

Basting

Use this method for transferring a design onto a fabric with a pile, such as velvet.

1 Pin the tracing in place on the fabric. Using a contrasting thread and small stitches, baste along the lines of the design.
2 Remove the paper by tearing it away from the fabric carefully.

Dressmaker's carbon paper

Use this method on fabrics with very fine and even weave, without irregular slub threads. Do not use it if the design contains any fine detail, as the prick and pounce method is the only reliable one. The carbon paper is available in light colors for use on dark fabrics and vice versa. Simply place the carbon paper under your tracing in the correct position on the fabric and trace over the design with a sharp pencil.

Prick and pounce method

This method is the only reliable one for transferring designs with fine detail or where you are using fabric with irregular slub threads.

Basically, prick holes are made through the tracing paper along the lines of the design and the design is transferred to the fabric underneath by rubbing a mixture of "pounce" over the paper.

"Pounce" was originally a powder made from ground cuttlefish bone used as a wig powder in the eighteenth century, but nowadays it is made from powdered chalk for dark fabrics and powdered charcoal for light fabrics. Some chalks for pouncing can be obtained from a well-stocked notions department or store or alternatively you can use talcum powder. To apply the pounce, you need a felt pad which can be made by rolling up several thicknesses of felt and securing the roll with overcasting.

1 Place the tracing paper onto a folded towel or well-padded ironing board to give a good base for pricking the design.
2 Use a fine needle for smooth fine fabrics or designs with a lot of detail and a larger needle for heavier fabrics. Insert the eye of the needle into a cork to make it easier to handle.
3 Go over the lines of the design, pricking it with holes $\frac{1}{16}$ inch apart on fine fabrics and $\frac{1}{8}$ inch apart on heavier ones.
4 Pin the tracing in position on the embroidery fabric. It is advisable to weight the edges of the tracing with something heavy to prevent it from moving.
5 Using the felt pad, rub the pounce all over the paper. Lift off the paper carefully. When the paper is removed, the design shows up on the fabric as a series of fine dots where the pounce has penetrated the prick holes.
6 Paint in the lines of the design, using a fine brush and white poster paint mixed with a little blue or yellow to make the design clearer on a white or very light fabric. Water color paint can be used instead of poster paint but it does not give as clear an outline and is best for fine transparent fabrics. As you work the embroidery the paint can be flicked off with the point of a needle.

Transferring designs onto sheer fabrics

1 Trace the design onto paper using a hard pencil or non-smudging ink. Check whether the tracing shows through the fabric, and if necessary go over the design again with white poster paint or a light crayon.
2 Place the fabric over the tracing and weight down to prevent it moving. Paint over the lines of the design, using a fine brush and poster or water color paint as in the prick and pounce method.

Transferring designs to canvas

For simple designs use the basting method, and for more complicated designs place the canvas over the tracing and trace the outline with waterproof ink.

Transferring designs using the prick and pounce method.

Making the prick holes through the tracing paper.

Using the felt pad, rub the pounce all over the paper.

Finally, paint in the lines of the design.

Enlarging and reducing designs

Whether you are using your own design or some pattern or illustration which you have copied, you will often need to enlarge or reduce it to fit the size you need. This is easy to do. To enlarge, divide the design into little squares, then copy it onto the same number of larger squares; and to reduce, divide the design in just the same way, then copy it onto smaller squares.

The simplest way of doing this in order to avoid marking the original design, and also to save the trouble of drawing out lots of little squares, is to transfer the design onto graph paper. To do this, you can either trace it directly, if the graph paper is thin enough, or use tracing paper and work the following way:

1 Trace the design onto tracing paper.

2 Lay this over graph paper. If you can see the squares clearly through the tracing paper, stick it down with clear tape, taking care that the tracing paper lies flat. This way, you can re-use the graph paper.

3 If, however, you cannot see the squares clearly through the tracing, transfer the design to the graph paper either with carbon paper (dressmaker's carbon is fine) or by shading the back of the tracing paper with a soft pencil and drawing firmly over the design with a ballpoint.

4 Draw a rectangle to enclose the design. This will be divided into a certain number of squares by the graph paper. If you are using plain paper you must, at this point, divide the rectangle by marking off each side and joining up the marks to make a lot of small squares. It is helpful to number

these for reference.

4 Draw, preferably on tracing paper as before, a second rectangle to the size you want the finished design and in the same proportions as the first one. Do this by tracing two adjacent sides of the first rectangle and the diagonal from where they meet. Extend them as much as you need and then draw in the other sides of the second rectangle. Divide this into the same number of squares as the smaller one. A backing sheet of graph paper will make this process easier.

6 Carefully copy the design square by square. If you have to copy a flowing, curved line across several squares, mark the points at which it crosses the squares and then join them up in one flowing movement.

1 Draw the design onto tracing paper.
2 Lay the tracing paper over graph paper.
3 Draw a rectangle to enclose the design and number the squares in it.
4 Draw the second rectangle by tracing two sides and a diagonal from the first (shown in red). Extend as needed.
5 Transfer the design square by square until it is completed.

SIMPLE STITCHES
Line and straight stitches

A knowledge of basic stitchery makes embroidery a creative and stimulating hobby, and it is essential if you intend to create your own individual embroideries. Probably the simplest stitches with which to start are line, or straight, stitches. These are illustrated below and can be used for any of the designs shown, using the tracing overleaf. A basic guide to these elementary stitches can be found for easy reference in the section on the essential stitches.

Basic stitches

Running stitch
Make the stitches on the right side the same length as those on the wrong side.

Laced running stitch
This can be effective using either the same or contrasting yarn. Use a tapestry needle and thread it in and out of the running stitches without catching in the cloth. This lacing can be used with other stitches.

Backstitch
Bring the needle through to the right side of the fabric and make a small stitch backward. Bring the needle through again a little in front of the first stitch and make

another stitch backward to make a continuous line.

Stem stitch
Make a sloping stitch along the line of the design, and then take the needle back and bring it through again about halfway along the previous stitch.

Cable stitch
Work lower stitch A on line of design, as shown; then work upper stitch B in same way with yarn above needle.

All smiles at bedtime with a beaming Mister Moon nightdress

A simple design in a solid color is made demurely pretty with a few motifs

A subtle use of an ice cream cone motif gives this blouse a distinctive look.

Motifs to use on their own or in groups. Trace the motifs from the page, transfer them to the fabric, then embroider them in pretty colors, using any of the straight stitches illustrated

Satin stitches

Although satin stitch is essentially a simple over-and-over stitch, skill is required to produce the beautiful satiny effect that its name implies. It is a surprisingly versatile stitch and, as it imposes no pattern of its own, it is invaluable for pictures where stitches of varying lengths and shades produce illusions of distance and depth. There are several variations, one of which is padded and gives the effect of an extra dimension. It is shown later in our stitch sample pages.

Satin stitch flower motif
This simple flower motif below is a good example of the effectiveness of the stitch when worked with long and short and split stitch. The motif can be worked in six-strand floss on a table napkin, dress or blouse.

Materials
6-strand floss (used with three strands in the needle) in six or seven colors. Allow 1 skein of yarn in each color for the design, although the exact amount you use will depend on how closely you stitch.

The design
1 Work the motif onto the corner of the napkin, placing it about 1 inch in from the sides.
2 The flowers of the design are worked in long and short stitch, the four upper leaves in satin stitch and the lowest leaf in split stitch. French knots decorate the centers.
3 The dotted line on the tracing pattern indicates the meeting point for stitches and suggests the position of the leaf vein. Transfer the design using tissue paper.
Begin by working the center flower, stitching from the inner line towards the outer edge. Work each half of each leaf in turn. Work flower color 4 first, then color 6, taking the stitches just into the edge of the leaves. Finally, work flower color 5. Make dots with a couple of small satin stitches or French knots at the centers.

▲ *A beautiful example of satin stitch worked in silk for picture making.*

▼ *The motif worked in cotton on a linen napkin.*

A delightful embroidery design "Panier de Fleurs" is featured on this pillow. It is worked in wool on canvas and satin stitch is used throughout. Designed by Jean-Yves Rocher for the D.M.C. "New Tapestry Collection".

Guatemalan motifs

Reversible satin stitch worked in bright colors in geometric patterns is characteristic of Guatemalan peasant embroidery as shown on the poncho and bag in the photograph. A similar motif can also look effective on the flap of a clutch bag and, since it is reversible, it will look as good when the bag is closed as when it is open.

Making a clutch bag

Make the clutch bag from a rectangle of loosely woven fabric, such as coarse linen. The minimum size of fabric for the motif shown is 18 inches × 9 inches.

Working the motif

Draw the motif (right) to scale (see earlier) and trace it onto tissue paper. Place the tracing in position on the top third of the rectangle. Baste over the lines indicating the color areas and then pull away the paper. Start stitching each area, working from the middle outward.

Finishing

Fold up the bottom third of the rectangle with wrong sides together to form the pocket and pin the sides. Trim the edge of the flap to within $\frac{1}{2}$ inch of the stitching. Cover the turnings and raw edge of the flap with a continuous length of bias binding machine stitched on both edges.

Above: Graph pattern for a Guatemalan motif. Work it in bright colors for a bag.

Each square = 1 inch square

Left: This poncho and bag are embroidered with satin stitch in Guatemalan motifs

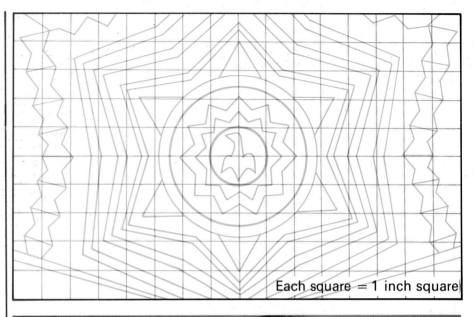

Each square = 1 inch square

Chain stitches : continuous

Chain stitch has no single origin but can be traced to all parts of the world where ancient fabrics have been found. Chain stitch was found on basket-work from pre-dynastic Egypt (c.350 BC), on the earliest surviving Egyptian textiles, in graves in the Crimea dating from the 4th century BC and on some Chinese and Japanese textiles from the 7th and 8th centuries AD. The Chinese worked chain stitch with silk yarn on silk in a single line technique, widening or tightening the loop with a thread of uniform thickness to produce an effect of variable depths of color and shadow. Some of the finest examples worked with chain stitch alone, using silk thread on satin, have been found on 18th and 19th century Indian garments from Kutch.

In medieval western Europe the richest embroideries used more elaborate stitches and chain stitch appeared only on more humble objects. In 18th century England chain stitch was revived and widely used, often inspired by Chinese motifs to decorate silk coats and satin bedspreads. It appears independently in peasant work throughout the world.

Using chain stitch

Chain stitch worked in lines and curves is very versatile. The stitch can be worked large or small to give a fine or a bold outline. For its usual look the proportions should remain the same; as a rough guide the width should be two-thirds of the length of the stitch.

Chain stitch adapts well to tight curves and can be worked around and around partially to fill in areas.

Chain stitch

When worked, this stitch forms a chain of loops on the right side of the fabric and a line of back stitches at the back. Bring the needle through on the line of the design, hold a loop of the yarn under the left thumb and insert the needle close to where the yarn emerged. Bring the needle through a little further along the line of the design, and, with a loop of the yarn under the point of the needle, draw through. Continue in this way until the required length has been worked (see below).

Suitable yarns

Small stitches worked in a thick yarn give

▲ *Working a line of chain stitch.*

These designs are shown about one-third of their actual size, but they may be enlarged to the size you require.

This pretty butterfly picture would be ideal for a girl's bedspread or embroidered onto a dress or apron pocket.

An appropriate design for a beach bag or beach cover-up – a colorful landscape scene with rolling waves.

Brighten up plain table mats with this simple motif. All these designs are worked in Soft Embroidery Cotton.

a solid line, while larger stitches in fine yarn give an open stitch. Use these characteristics to their fullest advantage. Any of the finer yarns and threads previously mentioned are suitable for chain stitch but for quickly worked chain stitch use a thick embroidery yarn such as those shown below, on a large weave backing.

2 ply Crewel yarn: a twisted, matte wool. Use one or, more usually, several strands.
Tapestry yarn: a twisted, matte wool.
Sugar 'n Cream: a knitting and crochet cotton.
Knit-Cro-Sheen: a fine knitting and crochet cotton.
Rug Yarn: a twisted, matte yarn for using on rug canvas.

To work the designs

1 Choose your project – perhaps a T-shirt cotton jacket. Enlarge and transfer the design.

If you plan to use a thick yarn you will need a chenille needle. Do not, however, use heavy yarn for any cotton fabric, including denim. Floss or 1 strand of Crewel is the heaviest you can use to avoid puckering.
2 Follow the lines of the design with closely worked chain stitches until you have covered them all.

Flower bed pillow

Fabric required

Single thread evenweave linen, 26 threads per 1 inch, 14 in × 14 in.

You will also need

Soft Embroidery Cotton, 3 skeins purple, 4 skeins red, 4 skeins mauve, 5 skeins lilac, 6 skeins light green, 6 skeins dark green, 6 skeins orange.
Fabric for back of pillow 14 in × 14 in.
Square pillow 14 in × 14 in.

The design

1 Transfer the pattern on facing page centrally onto the linen.
2 Lightly mark a square $\frac{3}{4}$ inch in from outer edges with a soft pencil.
3 Work the design in fairly small chain stitch, working over 2 or 3 threads to make stitches uniform in length.
4 Work around the edge of the square in chain stitch and work two more squares of chain stitch just inside the first border.
5 Finish the pillow, allowing for $\frac{1}{2}$ inch seams all around.

This flower bed design is set off well by a natural-colored background.

Tracing pattern for pillow

Detached chain stitch

Although chain stitches can be used continuously they can also be used as separate stitches and arranged to form flower or leaf shapes. This is known as lazy daisy or detached chain stitch. The stitches may be worked in any size you desire, but remember, if the stitches are very long they will catch easily and therefore are not suitable for everyday articles of clothing.

Needlework canvas

This is an embroidery fabric woven in even blocks of cotton strands separated by holes through which the needle is drawn. The number of holes per inch vary: 6 holes per inch have been used here and embroidery worked on this scale grows quickly. Penelope Binca and Panama canvas are examples of this type of embroidery fabric. The canvas is also available in smaller gauge for finer work. This is most often used for making pillows, table linen, chairbacks or stool tops.

After care

Wash in warm water and pure soap. Squeeze the fabric gently in the soapy water. Rinse thoroughly in warm water and squeeze gently by hand to remove excess water. Leave the fabric on a towel, lying flat, until it is half-dry. Press on the wrong side, using a moderately hot iron, working from the center outward and not allowing the weight of the iron to rest on the embroidered sections until the fabric is completely dry. If desired, you may also have the fabric dry cleaned.

Basic stitches

Detached chain or lazy daisy stitch

Make a chain stitch and instead of re- inserting the needle inside the loop, make a tiny stitch over the loop to hold it in place (A). Leave a space and bring the needle out again to begin the next stitch. Work the lazy daisy stitch in the same way as for the detached chain but position the stitches to form a flower shape (B).

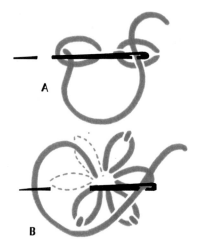

Lazy daisy stitch pillow

The flowers on this design are meant to be worked in a random fashion, therefore embroider the largest flowers first, spacing them out, and then fill the spaces in between with the smaller flowers. In the remaining spaces work the tiny four-petaled flowers and either bunches of, or single, leaves.

Fabric required

14 in square of cotton mesh, 6 holes per inch.

You will also need

11 skeins of embroidery wool in 11 different colors.
Tapestry needle No. 18.
Material for back of pillow cover, 14 inches square.
Pillow form, 13 inches square.

Working the embroidery

1 Work the desired number of flowers over the fabric, leaving a 1 inch border un-worked. To define the edge of the pillow work a border of leaves 1 inch in from the edge. Vary the height of the leaves so that they frame the flowers.
Note While working with the wool it is important to twist it to the right to keep the ply tightly twisted, thus being able to get a clean line to the design. Work the larger flowers one at a time.
2 Leave the ends of yarn on the wrong side and, sew them in neatly on the back

This colorful pillow displays a random pattern of flowers in detached chain stitch.

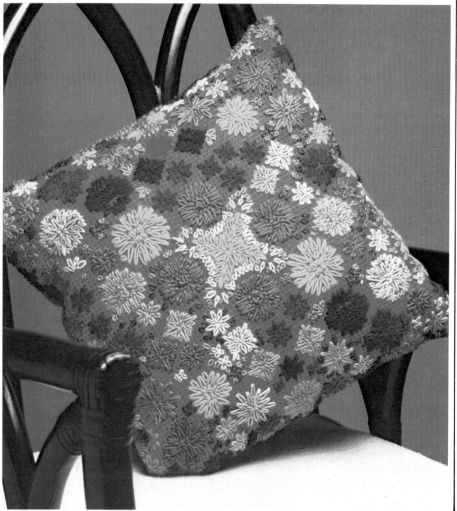

when you are finishing.

3 The detached chain stitches are held in place in two ways; either by bringing the yarn over the loop through the same hole

1 Compact detached chain stitch.

(Figure 1) or by bringing the yarn over the loop, over one block and through the next hole (Figure 2).

2 Detached chain stitch with a stem.

Finishing

1 Fold the edges of the fabric to the wrong side, so that the border of leaves is close to the edge, and pin. Fold the back of the cover to the same size and shape and pin those edges to secure them. Pin the back and front together, wrong sides facing (see below). Slip stitch around three edges,

3 Pin with wrong sides together.

insert the pillow form and slip stitch neatly along the fourth side to complete the pillow.

2 The motifs show the variety of shapes that can be worked over a similar number of squares.

Each square of the fabric represents the number of blocks to be worked as, for example, if the petal covers three squares there are two holes skipped between the inserting and drawing out of the needle.

Bright and pale colors show up well against either dark brown or cream colored backgrounds. The motifs may be arranged to make a pattern the same as, or similar to, the one opposite, and they are only a sampling of the many you can work.

Chain stitch as a filling stitch

When using chain stitch as a filling stitch it is easiest to start off with designs that are fairly round. With these shapes it is easier to work around and around and to keep the lines of stitches close together. Once you have completed a few such designs you will be ready to go on to more irregular ones. When working a design which is filled in with closely packed stitches choose a medium-weight fabric of some type comparable in weight to that of the stitching. Also choose a color and texture which is suited to the design.

When filling in a shape, work the stitches around the outline of the shape, then, as you return to the starting point, bring the needle point just inside the first round of stitches so that the start of the second round is hardly visible when the work is completed (see below). Keep working around and around, completely covering the background, until the center is reached, then bring the needle over the last loop and draw the yarn through to the back. Fasten off.

Filled chain stitch can be made to look almost three-dimensional if you start along the outline with larger chain stitches and gradually make them smaller and smaller as you progress toward the center. However, if you want the surface of the fabric to be completely covered with embroidery it will be necessary to fill in the center of the outer chain stitches with detached chain stitches.

Yarn

To use chain stitch as a filling stitch it is important to select a yarn of proportionate thickness to the weight of the fabric, which is why 6-stranded floss is most appropriate. Before starting the embroidery, however, work a few stitches to find out how many strands you need to achieve a stitch size that will completely fill your pattern.

Pressing and stretching

When stitches are worked very close together the fabric sometimes becomes puckered because the gauge of the stitching is too tight. All embroidery should be pressed on the wrong side with a warm iron to give it a finished appearance, but if the fabric is distorted it must be pressed and stretched to make it smooth.

To press the embroidery

Pad a large flat surface with a blanket and ironing cloth or use a well-padded ironing board. Place the fabric on the ironing cloth, wrong side uppermost, and press with a damp cloth not allowing the weight of the iron to rest on the embroidery.

To stretch the fabric

Pad a board with clean, damp blotting paper or, if blotting paper is not available, lay the fabric over several thicknesses of damp, white cotton fabric. Place the fabric on the blotting paper, or substitute for it, right side up. Attach one edge of the fabric to the board with thumb tacks, aligning the horizontal strands with the edge of the board. Repeat on the opposite edge and at the sides, aligning the vertical strands with the edge of the board. If the sides of the board are not at right angles, use graph paper or lined blotting paper to obtain accurate stretching.

Leave to dry for at least 24 hours.

To work the iris design

The contrast between the nubbly, dull linen background and the lustrous stranded cotton makes the textural effect of this design very exciting. Note, too, how the narrow spacing between the random, horizontal lines integrates the background cloth with the embroidery; without these lines the embroidery would appear superimposed.

Size

The design should be enlarged from the illustration shown opposite to $6\frac{3}{4}$ inches × $8\frac{1}{2}$ inches.

Fabric required

A piece of natural colored linen-look fabric, 10 inches × $10\frac{1}{2}$ inches.

You will also need

6-strand floss, for flowers, 2 skeins of peacock blue and 2 skeins of natural; for leaves, 1 skein dark gray, 1 skein chestnut; for horizontal background lines, 1 skein beige; for buds, 1 skein cinnamon. 1 crewel needle.

Working the design

Transfer and enlarge the design shown on the opposite page. The stitches are all worked with two strands of the floss. While working it is important to remove any kinks from the strands so that they work smoothly together.

To use the design as a picture

Fray the top and bottom edges of the fabric and finish them with an overcast stitch to prevent any further fraying. The sides may be either frayed and overcast or turned under and hemmed. Mount the fabric on a colored cardboard background, leaving about a 1 inch border all around and set the finished piece in a picture frame.

To use the design as a pillow

Center the design on a piece of cloth about 13 inches × 16 inches and finish into a pillow 12 inches × 15 inches.

To use the design on a dress

Work the design directly onto the front of a basic woolen dress.

Right: This beautiful piece of embroidery is made up entirely of very small chain stitches, some worked around and around to make up the iris flowers and buds, and others in lines to represent the leaves and the background. Yarn: 6-strand floss. Designed by Shifrah Fram.

Bring the needle through just inside the first line of embroidery.

French knots and other stitches

For picture making choose a theme with bold and simple shapes. Break down the composition into stitch areas, fitting an appropriate stitch to the type of texture which will best express that portion. As you gain experience, you may want to attempt more detailed subjects with the texture provided by a greater variety of stitches, and most probably some of these invented by your own ingenuity.

Background

To start with choose a finely woven, natural-colored fabric. When you have become more confident you will be able to use more complex backgrounds which will play a part in the composition of the design with textures of the fabric as well as the stitching becoming an integral part of the picture.

Borders

If you wish to embroider a frame around a picture, choose one that is in keeping with the subject – a rose-festooned one as shown here – or a geometric border for a more modern picture. Remember, though, that many pictures look their best when set in the simplest of picture frames.

Yarn quantities

For a small picture, such as the one shown, one skein of each color is usually more than enough. However, if one color predominates, or if the stitches are very closely or thickly worked, an extra skein may be needed.

Apple blossom picture

The apple blossoms on the tree in the picture are superbly shown with the use of French knots. These are also used on the girl's dress and hair band shown. Bold straight stitches which lie flat are used for the trellis in front of the bushes. These add a little perspective and contrast in texture. The colors used are light to medium tones and give the whole picture a pretty, country air.

Trace the design onto tissue paper, being careful not to tear it. Lay the tissue paper over the fabric. Using sewing or basting thread and a fine needle, sew through the tissue paper and fabric with small running stitches around the outline to indicate the position of the areas to be embroidered.

Tear the tissue paper away. The stitches not hidden by the embroidery are removed when the embroidery is complete.

Fabric required

Piece of fabric 15 in × 12 in

You will also need

1 skein each of 6-strand floss in each of the following colors: brown, pale pink, rose pink, light green, mid green, sage green, golden brown, white.
1 ball pearl cotton No. 5 in two shades of brown and pale blue.
Small amount of gold lurex yarn for trellis.

The design

1 Enlarge the picture to measure 13 in × 10 in.
2 Using pearl cotton, work as follows: for the girl's dress, chain stitch and stem stitch.
Bark of tree and branches, stem stitch.
3 Using all strands of floss, work as follows:
for the apple blossom, flowers under tree, girl's hairband and part of her dress: closely worked, loose French knots, with a few knots over the branches of the tree.
Grass and flower leaves, random straight stitches.
Background bush, feather stitch.
Foreground bush, herringbone stitch outlined with stem stitch.
Girl's hair and feet, stem stitch.
Girl's hairband, French knots.
Girl's arms, backstitch.

The trellis

Using all strands of floss together, work a lattice, couching it with the gold lurex yarn. In front of the trellis work the flowers in French knots and the leaves in detached chain stitch.

The border

The border is made of herringbone stitch in floss with stem stitches worked in pearl cotton on each side.
Work the rosettes in stem stitch from the outside toward the center and add one or two French knots at the center of each.
Work leaves in detached chain stitch.
To finish off the picture, lay it right side downward on a well-padded ironing board.

cover with a damp cloth and press it lightly. When dry, mount the picture.

Basic stitches

French knots (Figure 1)

Bring the thread out at the required position, hold the thread down with the left thumb and wind it around the needle twice as in A. Still holding the thread firmly, twist the needle back to the starting point and insert it as close as possible to where the thread first emerged. Pull the thread through to the wrong side and secure.

Trellis stitch (Figure 2)

Lay threads along the lines of the design and, with another thread, tack down the intersections by making small stitches into the fabric.

Feather stitch (Figure 3)

Work in a vertical line. Bring the needle through to the right of the center line of the design and take a small stitch to the right as shown, catching the thread under the point of the needle. Continue making a series of stitches to the left and right of the design line, catching the thread under the needle.

Herringbone stitch (Figure 4)

Working from left to right, bring the needle through above the center line of the design and insert it below this line to the right, taking a small stitch to the left and keeping the thread above the needle. Insert the needle then on the upper line a little to the right, taking a small stitch to the left with the thread below the needle. Continue alternating these two movements.

Texture is created in this pretty picture
by the use of French knots for blossom
and couching for the trellis.

Cross stitch

Cross-stitch is one of the simplest and most ancient of all embroidery stitches. It dates back to the Coptic period and has been a form of peasant art for many centuries, always appearing in one form or another in various parts of the world. The best examples of this work come from the Slav countries of Eastern Europe where it has been used to adorn national dress. Cross-stitch can be exciting and absorbing to work and in Victorian times in Britain it was a popular pastime to make cross-stitch pictures, often wrongly named "samplers" (true samplers should consist of several stitches).

Many of these pictures were made by young girls and usually consisted of the alphabet, a text, the signature of the artist, her age and the date of working, all in minute cross-stitch.

How to use cross-stitch

Cross-stitch can be used for exciting designs on clothes, such as smocks, blouses, and dresses; as a decoration on bags, belts and slippers; and for the home on rugs, table linen, and curtains. Whether it is worked in an all-over design or simply in a border pattern depends on the size of the item, the background fabric and on the design being worked.

The design

Because of the geometrical nature of the stitch, it looks its best when the design is formal and has a repeating pattern, such as shown on the border in the photograph. The shape of the spaces between the areas is as important as those areas filled with the stitch. Often main areas are left un-worked and the spaces suggest detail – a technique known as "voiding" – which is the main characteristic of another form of cross-stitch, called "Assisi work" (shown later).

The colors

Cross-stitch is usually worked in colors – usually very bright – which contrast with the background fabric, and the interplay of the colors you choose is all-important. It is often more effective to use several tones of one color (as in the design shown in the photograph) rather than introducing completely different colors.

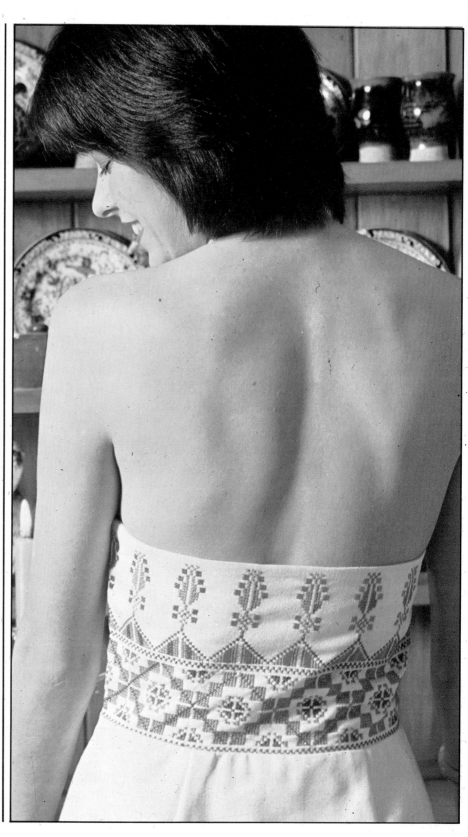

Planning your design

Although it is possible to buy transfers of cross-stitch patterns to print onto fabric, it is much more satisfying to use an evenly woven fabric and make up your own designs.

To plan your design, draw it first onto graph paper, using different colored pencils or different symbols to represent each color, with one square representing one stitch. When working from the graph each square may be considered as consisting of one or more threads, which remains standard throughout the work.

A unit of three threads usually makes a good average size cross, each stitch being made by counting three threads along the fabric and then three threads up.

By reducing or increasing the number of threads in the units – or by using fabric with fewer or more threads to the inch.

It is important in working cross-stitch that the counting of both stitches and threads must be accurate, and that if you are using a transfer it is necessary to be sure that the lines of the crosses lie on the weave of the fabric.

The fabric

Even-weave fabrics with threads which are easy to count are obviously the best to use for cross-stitch and besides the traditional embroidery linens you can also use hopsacking "Hardanger" cotton and many synthetic home furnishings fabrics. Checked fabrics can also be used even if the weave is uneven as the size of the crosses can be determined by the size of the checks.

The threads

Any threads – cotton, silk, linen or wool – can be used provided that they are suitable in weight to the background fabric. A coarse fabric needs a thread of heavier weight, while a fine fabric needs lighter threads.

Variety can be introduced by using threads of different textures for example, a thicker thread can be used to add depth and relief to your design.

The stitches

Cross-stitch is formed by two diagonal stitches, crossing in the center. There are two basic methods in which it can be worked, either by making one complete stitch at a time or by making a row of single diagonal stitches in one direction, then completing the stitch on the return row.

It is important that the upper half of the stitch always lies in the same direction if an even and regular effect is to be achieved. Traditionally the upper stitch should slope from bottom left to top right.

Combining cross-stitch

While there are numerous variations of cross-stitch which are used in other methods of embroidery, the stitch which is most often worked with regular cross-stitch is Holbein, or double running stitch. This is a small line stitch which is used to break up a mass of cross-stitch pattern and to lighten the texture. It produces a light filigree effect and is always worked in two steps.

The first step is worked along the required outline in running stitches which are of equal length to the spaces left between them. The work is then turned for the next step when the spaces left between the first stitches are filled in, thus forming a solid row. To keep the second line of stitches straight and even, bring the needle out of the fabric just below the stitch that was made in the first step, but still using the same hole of the fabric.

The design

The design shown in the photograph is made up of two simple repeat motifs and it can easily be adjusted to make borders for other garments (see chart below).

The top motif is 2 inches wide × 3¼ inches high. The border motif is 2¾ inches wide × 3⅛ inches high.

Below: Tracing pattern for the design illustrated opposite.

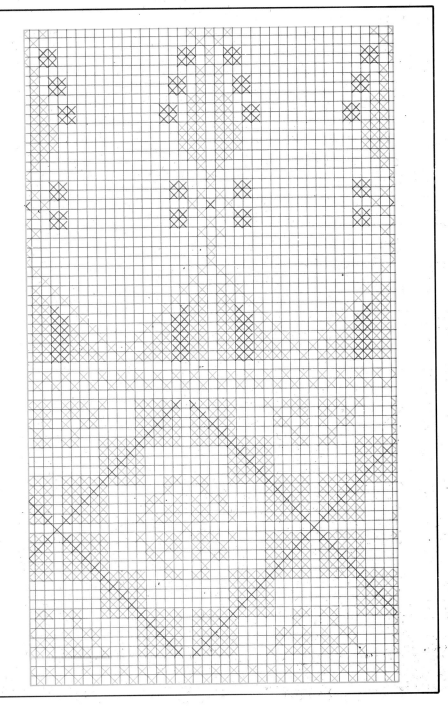

Cross-stitch motif

The photograph opposite shows a charming example of the kind of pictorial "sampler" worked by our forebears when they were children. Notice how the spaces between stitches are used to suggest features. If you do not wish to make a complete item from even-weave fabric, you could work the embroidery only on it, cut round leaving a margin of about ½ inch and apply it as a patch onto the finished item.

Fabric required

The motifs shown worked individually were done in stranded cotton on linen fabric. Alternatively, you could work in wool to brighten up a favorite cardigan or pullover.

You will also need

Remnants of stranded cotton or knitting wool in various colors. Try to match the weight of the yarn to the background using six strands of cotton or a sports yarn on a heavy background.

The design

1 Working over two or three threads of the fabric, work the stitches in the appropriate shades as shown in the charts. Darn all ends neatly through the backs of the stitches on the wrong side.
2 The size of the motif will of course vary, according to the weave of the background.
3 On a fabric with 19 threads per 1 inch for example, the cow motif would be about 4½ inches by 2 inches when each stitch is worked over two threads.
On a knitted background, work over a unit of one or two knitted stitches counted vertically and horizontally.

Basic cross-stitch

To work cross-stitch in two steps, bring the needle through on the lower right line of the cross and insert it at the top left line of the cross. Take a straight stitch along the wrong side of the fabric and bring the needle through on the lower right line of

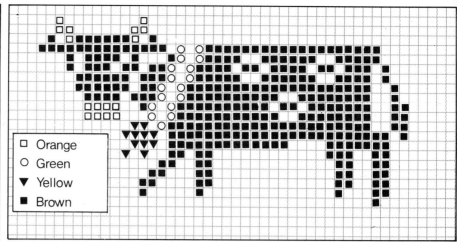

Legend:
□ Orange
○ Green
▼ Yellow
■ Brown

Working chart for the cow. Each square represents one cross-stitch.

The cow worked on linen with 19 threads per inch. Each stitch is over two threads.

the next stitch. Continue to the end of the row in this way (Figure 1a). To complete the stitch, work from left to right now in a similar way (Figure 1b).

Outlines and single stitches

To work cross-stitch individually, start as above but complete the cross each time

(Figure 2) before beginning the next stitch. Pass the thread on the wrong side of the fabric to the lower right line of the position of the next and subsequent stitches.

Holbein stitch

Working from right to left, work a row of running stitch, making the stitches and spaces the same length as the crosses. To complete the stitch, work from right to left, filling in the spaces left in the first row (Figure 3).

1. Two-step stitch.

2. Individually worked stitches.

3. Completing Holbein stitch.

Work this charming cross-stitch picture for a nursery or abstract the motifs and use them individually.

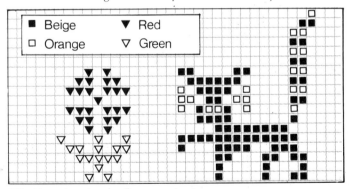

| ■ Beige | ▼ Red |
| □ Orange | ▽ Green |

Working chart for the flower and cat.

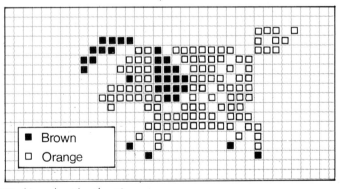

| ■ Brown |
| □ Orange |

Working chart for the pig.

The cat worked on linen as above.

The pig worked on linen as above.

Cross stitch alphabet

Cross-stitch has long been a favorite for embroidered lettering and monograms because it is quick and easy to work. No preliminary outline or transfer is needed when an evenweave fabric is used for the background because the fabric threads can be counted to form each letter.

Although cross-stitch designs based on counting threads are necessarily geometric in formation, still they leave plenty of opportunity for embellishment, as shown by the alphabet in the photograph. These letters have been worked in a modern version of the popular Victorian sampler, but you can easily extract the appropriate letters from the chart and use them individually to give a personal finish to your table linen or sheets, or you could combine them to form a monogram to decorate the pocket of a dress or the flap of a bag.

Working the alphabet

1 The alphabet in the photograph is worked on an evenweave cotton with 18 threads to 1 inch in 6-strand embroidery floss, using three strands throughout.
2 Each stitch is worked over one thread of the fabric and the letters are about 1¼ inches high.

Enlarging the letters

If you just want to double the size of the letters – and this means increasing their width too – you can work the stitches over two threads of the fabric.

Alternatively, you can work four stitches for every one stitch indicated on the chart, or if you do not want the increase to be that great, you can work the stitches over two threads but on a finer weave fabric.

Reducing the letters

The only method of reducing the size of the letters in proportion is to use a finer weave fabric.

Monograms

Composite intertwined initials are fun to plan and work. The initials may be arranged so that the base lines are level or you could place them diagonally.

Sketch out your monogram on graph paper before you start work so that you can see how the initials link and where they will have stitches in common.

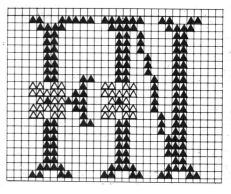

Above: Combined initials for a monogram.
Left: Chart for alphabet.

ABCDEFG
HIJKLMN
OPQRSTU
VWXYZ

FIRST PROJECTS
Simple peasant design

This beautiful embroidery design is worked with the simplest of stitches. The beginner will be able to work the design after following the previous few chapters – and the experienced embroiderer will have no difficulty at all. The design is suitable for a garment with yoke and sleeves.

To work the embroidery
Materials required
D.M.C. 6-strand floss: 3 skeins each of 666 turkey red, 604 rose pink, 553 violet, 3325 cobalt blue, 986 forest green, 3348 moss green, 972 amber gold.
Crewel needles No. 5 and 7.

Placing the motifs
The tracing pattern gives half the design used on the yoke with the broken lines indicating the fold. The section within the dotted outline gives half the design used on the sleeve.

Mark center-front of the blouse yoke with a line of basting stitches. Placing the fold line to center-front, trace the motif onto the right hand side of the yoke. Reverse and trace onto the left hand side. Trace section given within the dotted outline onto sleeves, approximately 5 inches from cuff. Repeat in reverse to complete the design as shown.

Method of working
Work the embroidery, following diagram 1 and number key. Use 6 strands of floss and No.7 needle for the French knots and 3 strands with No.5 needle for the remainder.

Most of the design is worked in simple satin stitch, stem stitch and French knots, with the centers of the flowers in spider's web filling stitch. Work this as shown in diagram 2. Work nine straight stitches on each side of the fly stitch tail, into the center of the circle. This divides the circle into nine equal sections and separates the spokes from the foundation of the web. Weave over and under the spokes until the circle is filled.

Spider's Web Filling Stitch

30

KEY TO DIAGRAM

1 — 666

2 — 604

3 — 553

4 — 3325   Satin stitch

5 — 986

6 — 3348

7 — 972

8 — 553

9 — 986   Stem stitch

10 — 3348

11 — 972

12 — 972   Spider's Web Filling Stitch

13 — 972   French Knots

A magnificent dragon

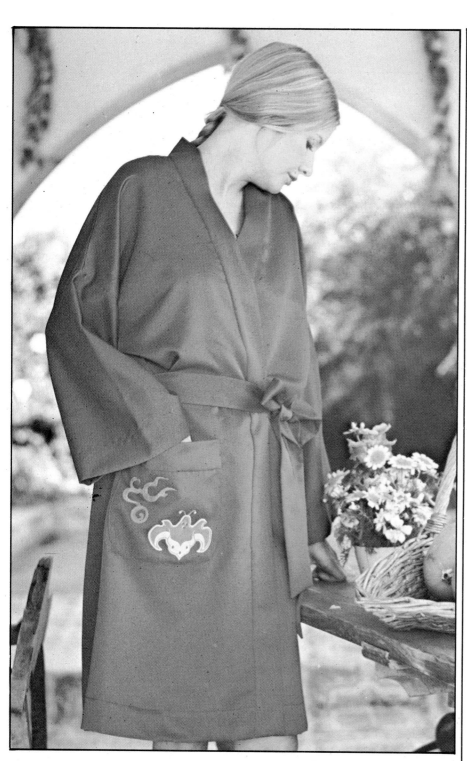

Fabric required
Length of emerald green fabric.

You will also need
D.M.C. 6-stranded floss in the following colors and quantities: 2 skeins each 992 jade and 725 amber gold; 1 skein each 797 cobalt blue; 993 and 991 jade; 704 and 700 grass green; 973 buttercup; 745 gorse yellow; 726 and 781 amber gold; 606 flame.
For alternative thread use D.M.C. Pearl Cotton No. 8 in the same colors.
McCall kimono pattern No. 3738.
Crewel needle No. 8.

The design
1 Lay out the pattern pieces on the fabric as directed in the pattern. Do not cut out the back and pocket pieces, but mark the cutting line on the fabric with either small basting stitches or with a tracing wheel and dressmakers' carbon paper. This is done to prevent the embroidery from pulling and possibly pulling the fabric out of shape.
2 Enlarge the design onto graph paper and transfer it onto the fabric. To do this either use an embroidery transfer pencil or trace the design onto tissue paper and sew it to the fabric with small basting stitches along the lines of the design, tearing the paper away afterwards.
3 Position the dragon on the back of the kimono 3 inches from the neck edge. The bat and pearl should be placed centrally on the pocket.

To work the embroidery
1 Use two strands of floss in the needle throughout. Follow the diagram and stitch key to work the embroidery. All parts similar to the numbered parts are worked in the same color and stitch.
2 To complete the dragon, work a French knot in the center of each eye on top of the satin stitch.

To make the kimono
1 Press the embroidery on the wrong side under a damp cloth.
2 Lay the pattern pieces on the embroidered back and pocket pieces. Check that the outlines of the pattern on the fabric have not been distorted by the embroidery. Adjust if necessary. Finish the kimono as directed by the pattern.

In China the dragon is regarded as the lord of all animals, a rain bringer and symbol of the highest intelligence. This magnificent dragon, embroidered on the back of an emerald green kimono, is chasing a flaming pearl, another popular Chinese symbol which represents the spring moon, herald of the fertile rainy season. A bat, symbol of happiness, is worked on the pocket of the kimono. Either use the design as we have here, or enlarge it and use it for a pillow or wallhanging.

Satin stitch.

Chain stitch.

Stem stitch.

Long and short stitch.

A

B

French knot.

33

Graph pattern for dragon design

each square = 1 inch square

Stitch key

Circles and spirals

Detached chain stitch.

Buttonhole stitch.

Chain stitch.

The colorful design on this pillow is based on a theme of circles. A vibrant range of colors and a few simple stitches combine to make this attractive pillow. A striking effect could be achieved by matching one embroidered pillow with others in plain fabrics chosen to pick up the embroidery thread colors.

Fabric required
17in squares of heavy cotton.

You will also need
16in square pillow form.
Crewel needles, No. 6 and No. 7.
Contrasting bias binding.

Yarn
D.M.C. 6-strand floss in the following colors and quantities: 1 skein each 796 indigo; 3326 magenta; 553 violet; 611 bark; 793 delphinium; 3024 tawny beige; 778 muted pink; 794 periwinkle; 825 king-fisher.

The design
Work the chain stitch flowers with three strands of floss. Stitch in a spiral from the outer edge to the center. The violet flowers are worked in a long detached chain stitch angled toward the center point. Work a smaller second stitch within each petal. The little flowers in the delphinium are made with closely stitched buttonhole wheels, using four strands in the needle.

To finish the pillow
Press the embroidery face down over a thick pad. Decorate the edges with a bias binding piping. Match it to one of the colors in the embroidery. Pin the two pillow pieces, right sides together, with the folded bias binding between the two layers and the fold of the binding facing into the center. Stitch three sides together through all layers. On the fourth side, stitch the binding to the seam line of the embroidered square. Turn the piece to the right side and press. Insert the pillow form and close with an overcast stitch, with a zipper or with snap fasteners.

Tracing pattern for flower bed pillow

Color Key
1. 796 indigo
2. 3326 magenta
3. 553 violet
4. 611 bark
5. 793 delphinium
6. 3024 tawny beige
7. 778 muted pink
8. 794 periwinkle
9. 825 kingfisher

Continue outer leaf pattern
to match opposite side

Working a family tree

Each square =
1 inch square

The design for the family tree shown here is reduced by half. Alter the design to accomodate a larger or smaller family.

One of the best ways of using stitches recently learned is to make up a sampler. This family tree uses four simple stitches, all illustrated on the previous pages and will make a beautiful and very personal addition to your home.

This adaptable embroidered version of a family tree was worked by Mrs Mary Pilcher for her grandson Robin (at the top of the tree), who is the fifth generation of Pilchers shown.

This family tree was worked as a present for Robin's second birthday, but a family tree for your own family would make an equally appropriate wedding or christening gift. The number of branches and sprigs will, of course, vary with the size of the family represented and also with the degree of lineage shown.

For your own tree, choose the fabric and colors that you like, remembering that the more personal the choice, the more your embroidered family tree will mean to you and to those who will, in time, inherit it.

Be sure to date your tree too, as Mrs Pilcher has done, because one day some member of a future generation will regard it with pride as a family heirloom.

Size
10 inches by $15\frac{3}{4}$ inches.
With the dimensions of the mounting board used as a frame, 13 inches by $18\frac{3}{4}$ inches.

Fabric required
$\frac{1}{2}$ yard ivory colored linen
$\frac{1}{2}$ yard of textured linen or similar fabric in contrasting color

You will also need
Anchor Stranded Cotton in the following colors, 0268 medium moss green, 0269 dark moss green, 0280 medium muscat green, 0281 dark muscat green, 0308 amber gold, 0358 medium peat brown, 0359 dark peat brown, 0326 dark orange, 0332 flame.
Shelf paper or similar grease-proof or tracing paper, each sheet measuring approximately 10 inches by 14 inches.
Two pieces heavy cardboard for mounting, one measuring 10 inches by $15\frac{3}{4}$ inches and the other 13 inches by $18\frac{3}{4}$ inches.
2 yards rickrack trim.
Rubber adhesive.
$2\frac{1}{2}$ yards masking tape.

The design
Planning the design
1 Use the design given as a basic pattern for your own family tree, adjusting it as required. Work out whatever changes are necessary on a sheet of shelf paper, doing

this preliminary work in pencil so that changes can be easily made.

2 Fold the sheet of shelf paper in half lengthwise, making a sharp crease. Open it out and use the center, vertical fold as a guide line for the tree trunk. Draw in the tree trunk with a pencil. Make a list of the baby's relations or members of the family to be included, and decide how many branches the tree will need. If working the tree for a baby, the names of his parents and grandparents will be embroidered down the main trunk of the tree and great aunts, uncles and cousins on the side branches.

3 Additional side branches can be worked in if necessary and a strategically placed flower or leaf will balance the design if it becomes asymmetrical. After adjusting the design of the tree, outline it in ink. Underline the names to be worked in ink, but omit the names on this pattern.

Transferring the design

1 Fold the tracing paper vertically as above, open it out and place over the design, matching the center folds. Trace all the lines you will need for the embroidery.

2 Fold the background material in half lengthwise, making certain the fold is along the straight grain of the fabric. Put a few pins along the center fold as a guideline. Place the tracing of the design over the material, matching the folds, then pin and baste them together.

3 With small basting stitches baste along all the lines for embroidery, being careful to start and finish securely so that the basting threads won't pull out. Tear away the paper, leaving the basted design on the background fabric. These basting stitches are removed as the embroidery progresses by snipping the thread and pulling out a short length at a time.

To make the family tree

Follow the working chart and key for stitches and colors to be used in the design. The key also indicates the number of strands to be used in each area.

1 Use two pieces of heavy cardboard to mount the embroidered panel and frame it. The smaller piece measures 10 inches by $15\frac{3}{4}$ inches and the larger, 13 inches by $18\frac{3}{4}$ inches.

2 Place the smaller piece of cardboard on a table so that one side extends over the edge by a few inches. Lay the embroidery over it, right side up, centering the work as carefully as possible. Starting at the center of one side, feel the edge of the cardboard through the material with your left thumb and pin at 1 inch intervals. Stick the pins straight through the edge of the card-

Grass	outer row	chain stitch	2 strands	0268 med. moss green
	middle row	stem stitch	1 strand	0281 dk. muscat green
	inner rows (two)	stem stitch	1 strand	0280 med. muscat green
Tree trunk	outer row	stem stitch	3 strands	0359 dk. peat brown
	inner row	stem stitch	2 strands	0358 med. peat brown
	inner row	stem stitch	1 strand	0308 amber gold
Roots		stem stitch	3 strands	0359 dk. peat brown
		stem stitch	2 strands	0358 med. peat brown
		stem stitch	2 strands	0281 dk. muscat green
Flowers		detached chain stitch	2 strands	0332 flame
			2 strands	0326 dk. orange
Sun	center	stem stitch	1 strand	0308 amber gold
		stem stitch	1 strand	0332 flame
		stem stitch	1 strand	0326 dk. orange
	rays	open Cretan stitch	1 strand	0326 dk. orange
Leaves	outer row	stem stitch	3 strands	0269 dk. moss green
	center	open Cretan stitch	3 strands	0268 med. moss green
		open Cretan stitch	3 strands	0280 med. muscat green
		open Cretan stitch	3 strands	0281 dk. muscat green
Lettering		stem stitch	1 strand	0359 dk. peat brown
Underlining		stem stitch	1 strand	0326 dk. orange
Butterflies		stem stitch	3 strands	0308 amber gold
		French knots	3 strands	0308 amber gold

Detached chain stitch.

Stem stitch.

French knots.

Open Cretan stitch.

picture wire

small curtain ring

mystik tape

heavy cardboard

fabric edges

rickrack

textured background fabric

heavy cardboard

Rickrack is tucked down along the back edge of the panel to add a decorative trim.

Finish off the back of the completed panel with tape and curtain rings for hanging.

board, perpendicular to it. Turn the cardboard around, then pin along the opposite edge, pulling as tight as possible. Check to see that the embroidery is centered on the cardboard and that the grain of the fabric is straight in both directions; take the pins out and adjust if necessary. Now pin the third side and the fourth, so that the fabric is very tight but the embroidery is not distorted.

3 When you are quite certain that the embroidery is positioned correctly, turn the cardboard over and stick down the edges with rubber cement. Leave the pins in place until the cement is dry, then remove them and trim the corners.

4 Cover the larger piece of cardboard with the textured background fabric in the same way. Spread a small amount of rubber cement in the center of the material to join the two panels.

If rickrack trim is used, stick it down along the back edge of the smaller panel before joining. Glue the rickrack half way down one side of the panel, adjusting as necessary from the front. Make certain that a loop appears at each corner, stretching or easing the rickrack to make this possible. If you prefer not to frame the finished panel, cover the raw edges of the material on the back with masking tape. Slip a short length of tape through each of two small curtain rings and fix in place with masking tape. A length of picture wire can be extended between the two rings for hanging the panel.

THE ESSENTIAL STITCHES

Stitches can be divided into six main groups, according to their general method of construction, and as you become more expert you will see how they can be adapted to add interest and individuality to your work.

Line stitches
Stem stitch

This stitch is used principally as a line or outline stitch. Work from left to right taking small slanting stitches along the line of the design. The thread should always emerge on the left-hand side of the previous stitch and should be below the needle. Outline stitch is worked in the same way but the thread should be above the needle.

Backstitch

Work from right to left. Bring the thread through the stitch line, take a small stitch back into fabric and bring out the needle the same distance in front of the first stitch. To repeat, insert the needle into the fabric at the point of the first stitch.

Split stitch

This can be used as a line stitch and a filling stitch when worked closely together. Work from left to right. Bring the thread through the stitch line and make a small stitch with the needle pointing backward.

Bring the needle up piercing the working thread and splitting it.

Running stitch

Work from right to left. Insert the needle into the fabric making stitches of equal length above and below the fabric so that on both sides the stitches and spaces are of equal length.

Pekinese stitch

Work a row of backstitch, then interlace it with a different, preferably heavier thread, for contrast. The bottom part of the interlacing should lie flat, leaving a looped edge on the upper side of the backstitch.

Flat or filling stitches
Satin stitch

This is a close straight stitch which is usually used as a filling stitch. The stitches

should be flat and even on the right side of the work.

Herringbone stitch

Work from bottom left to upper right. Bring the needle out on the lower line at left and insert at top right, making a small stitch to the left and keeping the thread below the needle. Repeat, making a small stitch at bottom and top as you progress. The stitch can be laced in a variety of ways with ribbon or thread and can be as narrow or as wide as desired.

Encroaching satin stitch

This is another useful way of shading. Work the tops of the stitches in the second and subsequent rows in between the bases of the stitches in the row above.

Padded satin stitch

For small surfaces in a design and to give additional texture, some parts may be padded with rows of small running stitches, chain or split stitch before the satin stitch is worked. To make a neat contour you can outline the edge first with split stitch and then work satin stitch over the whole shape.

Raised satin stitch

This is effective for small parts of pictures where you want a three-dimensional effect. Start in the same way as for padded satin stitch across the shape. Then work a second layer at right angles to the first one.

Chevron stitch

Work from bottom left to top right and from top to bottom alternately, making small backstitches. Bring out the needle halfway along each backstitch, keeping the thread alternately above and below the needle as the stitch progresses.

Fishbone stitch

This is a useful filling stitch which should be kept even and compact. Note the small straight stitch at the beginning which is not repeated. Bring the thread through at A and make a small straight vertical stitch along the center line of the shape. Bring the thread through again at B and make a sloping stitch across the center line at the base of the first stitch. Bring the thread through at C and make a similar sloping

stitch to overlap the previous stitch. Continue working alternately on each side until the shape is filled.

Looped stitches

This group of stitches shows only some of the many which are formed by looping thread around a needle.

Buttonhole stitch

Work from left to right, starting on the bottom line. Insert the needle into the fabric above the line at desired distance, take a straight downward stitch, and bring out the needle with the thread under it. Pull up the stitch to form a loop and repeat the process. Once the basic method of working the stitch is mastered, the variations such as closed, up and down and knotted buttonhole stitch are not difficult.

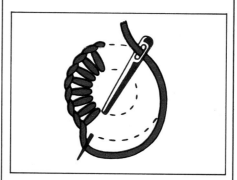

Vandyke stitch

This stitch closely worked will form a thick plaited line but it can also be used as a filling stitch. It must be worked very evenly to form a good plait. Bring the thread through at A. Take a small horizontal stitch at B and insert the needle at C. Bring the thread through at D. Without piercing the fabric, pass the needle under the crossed threads at B and insert at E. Do not pull the stitches too tightly or the regularity of the center plait will be lost.

Cretan stitch

A most useful and versatile stitch with a number of uses when worked closely or

openly and irregularly. Work from left to right. Bring the needle through on the left-hand side, take a small stitch on lower line with the needle pointing upward and the thread behind it. Take a stitch on the upper line with the thread under the needle. Repeat movements.

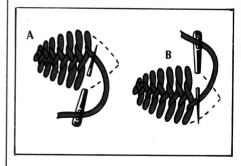

Loop stitch

This is similar to Vandyke stitch but its effect is not so heavy and the two should not be confused. Work from right to left. Start at center of the stitching line, take the thread through at A and insert at B, bring through at C immediately below B. Keep the thread to the left and under the needle, pass the needle under the first stitch without entering the fabric.

Feather stitch

This stitch gives a feathery effect but must be worked very evenly to prevent it becoming straggly. Bring out the needle at top center, hold the thread down with the left thumb, insert the needle a little to the right on the same level and take a small stitch down to the center, keeping the thread under the needle point.

Insert the needle again, this time a little to the left on the same level as the previous stitch and take a stitch to center, keeping the thread under the needle.

The design is completed by working these two movements alternately

Fly stitch

This can be worked closely as a line and either regularly or sparsely as a filling. Work from the left when using it horizontally and from the top when working on a vertical line. Bring the thread through at top left, hold it down with the left thumb, insert the needle to the right on the same level and take a small stitch down to the center with the thread below the needle. Pull through and insert the needle below the center stitch to hold the loop and bring it through in position to begin the next stitch.

Chain stitches

There are at least nine varieties of chain stitch and the simpler versions, such as ordinary chain, twisted chain and open chain, can be whipped, overcast or threaded.

Chain stitch

This is usually worked from top to bottom vertically and from right to left horizontally. Start by bringing the thread through at the top and inserting the needle again at the same place, forming a loop. (If you are working in the hand, you may find it easier to hold the loop down with your left thumb.) Take a small stitch forward, bringing the needle up through the loop and keeping the thread under the needle. Repeat the stitch, varying its length as desired.

Twisted chain stitch

This most useful stitch should be worked closely and evenly to produce a firm twisted line. Work as for ordinary chain

stitch but insert the needle just outside the last loop and at a slight angle to the stitching line with the thread below the point of the needle, as shown.

Open chain stitch

This must be worked evenly to prevent it from becoming very loose and uneven. Bring the needle through at A, hold down the thread and insert the needle at B, the desired width of the stitch, then bring the needle through at C, the desired depth of the stitch, leaving the loop thus formed slightly loose. Insert the needle now at D and, with the thread under the needle, bring it through for the next stitch. Secure the last loop with a small stitch at each side.

Heavy chain stitch

This makes a very firm close line. Start at the top and work down. Bring out the thread at point A and make a small vertical stitch. Bring the thread through at B and pass the needle under the vertical stitch without penetrating the fabric, using the eye of the needle, rather than the point, since this is easier. Insert the needle again at B and bring it out at C. Pass the needle under the vertical stitch and insert again at C. Continue forming stitches in this way, passing the needle under the two preceding loops.

Rosette chain

For this stitch to be effective with either thick or thin threads it must be worked evenly and closely, with no loose top edge. Work from right to left and bring the thread through at the right end of the upper line, then pass it to the left, holding it down with the left thumb. Insert the needle into the upper line a short distance from where it first emerged and bring it out on the lower line with the thread under the needle point. Draw the needle through the loop and, using the eye of the needle, pass it under the top edge of the stitch.

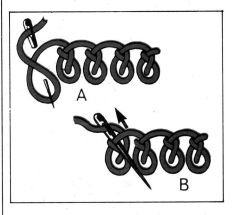

Wheatear

This is a simple stitch which combines straight stitches and a chain stitch. Work two straight stitches at A and B. Bring the thread through below these at C and pass the thread under the two straight stitches without penetrating the fabric. Insert the needle again at C, bring it through at D and repeat.

Knotted stitches

Some of the stitches in this group, such as French knots and bullion, are intended to be worked as single stitches while others are more suitable for use as line stitches.

French knots

Bring out the needle at the required position, hold the thread down with the left thumb and encircle the thread with the needle two or three times, depending on the thickness of the thread and the size of knot desired. Still holding the thread firmly, return the needle to the starting point and insert it very close to where the

43

thread emerged. Pull the thread through to the wrong side of the fabric and secure if working a single stitch or pass on to the position of the next stitch if you are working a group. It is a common error to insert the needle too far from the point where the stitch was started, making a loose, untidy knot.

Bullion stitch

The second part of this stitch is taken back over the first part so it is this first part which dictates the finished length of the stitch. Pick up a backstitch of the desired length, bringing the needle point out where it first emerged from the fabric. Wind the thread around the needle point as many times as required to equal the space of the backstitch, hold the wound thread down with your left thumb and pull the needle through. Still holding the wound thread, return the needle to where it was first inserted (see arrow) and pull through until the stitch lies flat.

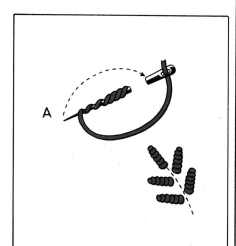

Coral stitch or knot

This is best worked as a firm line as it becomes weak and straggling if the knots are too far apart. Work from right to left or from top to bottom. Bring the thread out at the starting point and lay it along the line to be worked, holding it down with the left thumb. Take a small stitch under

the line where the knot is to be spaced (the thread lies on top of the needle as it enters the fabric) and pull through, taking the needle over the lower loop to form the knot.

Double knot

This is a slightly more complicated knot stitch. The knots should be spaced evenly and closely to obtain a beaded effect. Bring the thread through at A and take a small stitch across the line to be worked at B. Pass the needle downward under the stitch just made without penetrating the fabric, as at C. With the thread under the needle, pass it under the first stitch again as at D. Pull the thread through to form a knot.

Knotted cable chain

Work from right to left. Bring the thread through at A and place it along the line to be worked. With the thread under the needle, take a stitch at B (which is a coral knot). Pass the needle under the stitch between A and B without penetrating the fabric, as shown at C. With the thread under the needle, make a slanting stitch across the line of stitching at D, close to the coral knot. Pull the thread through to form a chain stitch.

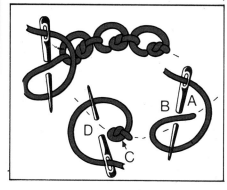

Composite stitches

These form a group which are usually worked on a foundation of satin stitch bars and they can be used as filling or line stitches. The satin stitch bars can be lengthened or shortened as desired.

Portuguese border stitch

Work the desired number of horizontal straight stitches (satin stitch bars). Working from the bottom upward, bring the thread through at the center and below the first bar (point A). Keeping the thread to the left of the needle take the thread over and under the first two bars, over the first two bars again and then under the second bar only without penetrating the fabric. With the thread now at B, work the second pair of stitches in a similar way and continue upward to the top of the row. Return to point A and work the second row of stitches up the foundation bars, keeping the thread to the right of the needle. Do not pull the surface stitches too tightly.

Raised chain band

If worked as a heavy line stitch it is advisable to use a finer thread for the foundation bar, but this should be of suitable weight to carry the chain stitch which can be in a heavier thread (for example 6-strand floss for the bars and soft embroidery cotton for the chain stitches). Work the desired number of satin stitch bars, then, starting at the top and working down, bring the needle through at A in the center of the first bar. Pass the needle up to the left and down to the right under the foundation bar, as shown, then through the chain loop thus formed. Repeat for the following stitches.

Raised stem band

This is worked in a similar way as for raised chain band but substituting stem stitch for chain stitch. The stem stitch can be worked from top to bottom but the effect is more even if worked from the bottom up.

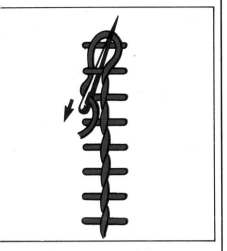

Woven band

This stitch is worked on evenly spaced foundation bars from the top down. You will require two needles with contrasting thread and you will obtain a better effect if one is shiny and the other dull, both in the same color, rather than with two contrasting colors. Bring both threads through at the top of the foundation bars with the lighter or silky thread to the left. Pass this thread under the first bar and leave it there. Take the darker or dull thread over the first bar, under the second bar and under the light thread. Leave the dark thread there and pass the light thread over the second bar, under the third bar and under the dark thread. Continue in this way to the end of the band. Begin each following row at the top. By altering the sequence of the contrasting thread, various patterns can be achieved.

Interlaced band

This stitch is composed of two rows of backstitch with an interlacing band. The distance between the backstitch rows depends on the thickness of the interlacing thread, and will be greater when using a thick thread. For the backstitch, the center of the stitches in the bottom row should be directly in line with the end of the stitches in the top row so that the interlacing can be worked evenly. Bring the lacing thread through at A and interlace through every stitch as shown.

Spider's web

This is a useful and decorative stitch of which there are two varieties.

Spider web, whipped Work an even number of equal or unequal length stitches radiating from a center point – six or eight stitches is the usual number. Bring the needle through the center. Working from right to left as you progress around the spokes of the web, work a backstitch over each spoke. Pass the needle under the next thread before working the backstitch over it. To finish off, take the thread down into the fabric immediately under a spoke and fasten off underneath. The spokes of the web can be completely filled in but a better effect is made by leaving some unworked with the spokes showing.

Woven spider's web or woven wheel

Work an uneven number of stitches radiating from a center point. Bring the needle up in the center and weave the thread over and under the spokes. This can be worked from left to right or vice versa. Finish off as for the backstitched web.

Couching

Couching a line means to lay a line of thread (heavy, light, thick or thin) on the fabric on the line of the design and stitch it down at regular intervals with another thread which may be in a contrasting color. The stitching must be evenly spaced.

Sheaf stitch

This is a useful stitch which can be used as a filling or as an isolated stitch. It can be worked at spaced intervals or closely grouped. It consists of three vertical satin stitches which are overcast with two horizontal satin stitches, worked with the head of the needle without penetrating the fabric.

ADVANCED STITCHERY
ASSISI WORK

Assisi work is basically a form of cross-stitch embroidery, although the principle of the work is reversed and the stitches form the background of the design while the basic designs are left unworked. (This technique is known as 'voiding'.)

As its name suggests, Assisi work originated in Italy. For centuries it has been used to decorate ecclesiastical linen and vestments, as well as peasant clothing and household linen. Today it can be used to decorate sheets and pillows, place mats and tablecloths, or it can form an unusual embroidery on a child's dress or on an accessory such as a bag or belt.

The designs

Traditionally the designs for Assisi work were formal and generally naturalistic; representing animals, birds or flowers in a stylized manner. Geometric designs were also often used.

Contemporary Assisi work can be inspired by designs from many sources such as mosaics, carvings, wrought iron work, screen walls, architectural details, geometric patterns and lettering.

Abstract shapes or stylized reversed initials can also look effective in a border or on the pocket of a dress.

Making your own design

The simplest way is to draw the design onto a graph, starting by outlining the motif in straight lines, following the lines on the graph and then filling in the background so that you can get an idea of the effect. As with cross-stitch (see earlier), each square on the graph should represent a unit or stitch. The basic stitch is then worked over three or four threads of an even-weave fabric.

The colors

The traditional colors for the embroidery fabric in Assisi work were either white or natural linen with the stitches worked in two colors – usually browns, blues or dark reds, outlined either in a darker tone of the same color or in black.

A contemporary color scheme could be dark blue or navy threads worked on a paler blue fabric or orange on yellow, although it is best not to mix colors for the stitchery.

Fabrics
Because all the stitches are worked over a specific number of threads, an even-weave fabric is essential, whether linen, cotton, wool or a synthetic home furnishings fabric.

Threads
Pearl cotton, coton à broder and linen threads of a suitable weight for the fabric can all be used for Assisi work.

Needles
Use tapestry needles of a suitable size for the fabric and thread.

Method
There are only two stitches used for this type of embroidery – cross-stitch for the background and Holbein (or double running) for the outlining of the motif, plus a

combination of both stitches for a repeating pattern.

Start by working the Holbein stitch around the outline, counting the threads carefully. Make the stitches about three threads long, with equal spaces. Work around any offshoots of the design, carrying the thread out to the end of the line and back again to the main outline.

On the completion of the first step the design may look rather disjointed and muddled, but with the second step the stitch gaps are filled in and the design begins to take form. When all the outlining is complete the background can be

filled in with cross-stitch. Either of the two methods of cross-stitch can be used although for large embroidered areas you may find it quicker to work it in two stages. Make sure that the upper stitch in each cross lies in the same direction and that you take the stitches right up to the outline in order to preserve the character of the work.

Adding a border
When the background is complete the embroidery should have a very solid appearance and quite often needs a small border to soften it slightly. This can be a small geometric repeating pattern in Holbein worked either side of the design.

Finishing the edges
Final hems should be narrow and unobtrusive in order not to detract from the work. On table linen a hemstitched hem usually works well, while on a dress, pocket or belt the work can be finished with an invisible hem.

Assisi work tablecloth

The design in Assisi work is achieved by working over counted threads on an evenweave fabric, with a yarn which should be of a similar thickness to the warp and weft threads of the fabric. The finer the weave, the more attractive the design will be.

The actual motifs are formed by outlining them first in Holbein (double running) stitch and then filling in the background area with cross-stitch. The fabric is thus left showing through the shape of the motifs. As the embroidery is worked over counted threads, the design has a stylized geometric look, and curves can only be indicated by stepped or diagonal stitches. If you wish to make up or adapt your own design, it is best to work it out on graph paper first (10 squares to 1 inch is suitable). Each square on the graph paper should represent one stitch and then, according to the fabric used, you can decide how many threads to work each stitch over. Most designs are repetitive and can be varied to suit the size desired. Figures 1 and 2 show two simple treatments of a flower form and figure 3 shows a stylized bird form.

Assisi work tablecloth
Size
44in square.

Fabric required
1⅓ yards of 54 inch wide cream evenweave fabric, 30 threads to 1 inch.

You will also need
Pearl Cotton No. 8 in the following colors and quantities: 3 balls 797 blue; 1 ball 310 black
Tapestry needle No. 24
Embroidery hoop

Placing the design
1 Trim the fabric to an exact square with 46 inch sides, cutting along the grain lines. Find the center by folding the fabric in half both horizontally and vertically and basting along the creases with a contrasting thread, following the grain. The point where the two lines meet marks the center of the cloth.

2 Turn under ¼ inch all around the edges and baste to prevent the fabric from fraying while you are working.

3 The chart gives just over half of one side of the square design in the center of the cloth. Each square represents one stitch worked over three threads of evenweave fabric. The center is indicated by the white arrow which should coincide with one of the lines of basting stitches. Start the Holbein stitch outline at the small black arrow 213 threads down from the crossed basting stitches, and follow the pattern as shown on the chart.

4 The design is repeated as a mirror image on the other half of the first side. Work the remaining three sides to correspond.

Working the outline
1 Work all the embroidery in a hoop. Embroider the entire outline of the bird and flower design first in Holbein stitch, using black Pearl Cotton. Holbein stitch is worked in two steps. The first row is formed by working running stitch over and under three threads of fabric, following the shape of the design. When this is completed, work back in the opposite direction, filling in the spaces left in the first row. The diagonal stitches are formed by counting three across and three down (or up as desired) and inserting the needle at this point. Work the lines of the pattern inside the motifs, as for example the bird's eye, at the same time as working the outline.

Working the background
1 When the black outline is completed, fill in the background with horizontal lines of cross-stitch, using blue Pearl Cotton. It is important to work all the stitches with the top half of the stitch facing the same way.

2 Continue each row as far as it will go and fill in any separate areas later. Since the back of the cloth should look as perfect as the front, the thread should not be carried over any of the unworked motifs.

3 Where the outline takes a diagonal direction, it may be necessary to use half a cross-stitch only in filling in the background. To finish, work the inner and outer borders in Holbein and cross-stitch as indicated on the chart, using blue Pearl Cotton.

Finishing
Press the embroidery on the wrong side. Turn under a ¾ inch hem all around, mitering the corners as shown in the diagram, and slip stitch in place. A more decorative hem can be worked if desired by withdrawing one or two threads around the edges of the cloth and finishing off with hem stitch.

As a finishing touch, repeat the Holbein and cross-stitch border about 3 inches from the edge of the cloth.

Stitch chart for Assisi work cloth

Figs 1, 2 Two simple treatments of a flower motif.

Fig 3 A basic bird motif is reversed and a simple outline added to create an effective design.

The Holbein stitch outline is worked in black Pearl Cotton and the cross-stitch background and the borders in blue Pearl Cotton.

Center of design

A

B

Cross-stitch.

Holbein or double running stitch.

Each square represents one stitch worked over three threads of fabric

BLACKWORK

Blackwork is a monochrome method of embroidery, and relies for effect on the contrasting tone values produced by varying the density of the pattern fillings and the weight of yarn used.

Blackwork became fashionable in England during the reign of Henry VIII when it was used mainly for the decoration of garments. Later it was also used to decorate household articles and home furnishings. Although its name derived from the method of working a geometric pattern in black silk or cotton threads on a white or cream background, any combination which gives a good contrast between dark thread and lighter fabric can be used. In the Tudor period it was frequently worked with a dark red silk on a cream fabric.

The fabric

Since blackwork is a counted thread method of embroidery, choose a fabric which is evenly woven and where the threads can be easily counted.

You could also use a heavy slubbed evenweave linen or cotton which will give a slightly uneven but attractive variation to the stitchery.

The threads and needles

You will need a selection of threads of all weights to provide the depth of tone and contrast in the stitchery. Machine Embroidery cotton No. 30, pure sewing silk, 6-strand floss, pearl cotton Nos. 5 and 8, coton à broder and matte embroidery thread (on a heavier fabric) are all suitable and some of the various types of lurex and metal threads can also be incorporated. You will need tapestry needles in a variety of sizes to suit the fabric and threads.

The stitches

The stitches are simple and mostly variations of backstitch. Holbein or double running stitch can also be used for building up a border pattern incorporating blackwork filling stitches.

The patterns

The basis of all blackwork patterns is a simple geometric design which can be adapted to the depth of tone desired either by using a heavier or lighter thread or by adding and subtracting additional straight stitches. The spacing of the pattern will also enable a lighter or darker tone to be achieved.

The traditional method of working blackwork was to use the patterns as fillings for shapes of flowers, birds or animals, with the shape outlined with a heavier thread. Today these heavy outlines are usually omitted.

If you are experimenting with blackwork, start by using one basic pattern, working it first over four threads of fabric and then altering the tone or size of the pattern by adding or subtracting part of it. Alternatively, you might work the pattern over a different number of threads.

The pattern shown below can be made to appear darker, for example, by working a small cross-stitch in the center of each shape, or lighter in tone if each alternate small cross was omitted.

Blackwork chessboard

The chessboard illustrated over, is in fact a blackwork sampler, showing a variety of filling patterns. By working the patterns in alternate squares with blank squares in between, the sampler becomes an attractive and unusual chessboard as well as a permanent reference for the various patterns.

The sampler was stretched over plywood, covered in glass to keep it clean and give a good playing surface for chess, and then framed.

Size

The materials given below are for a chessboard 16 inches square, excluding the border, with 2 inch individual squares.

Right: A simple design in blackwork ideal to form a border.
Below: A complex arrangement of blackwork stitches used to create an abstract design for a wallhanging or picture.

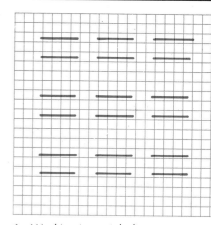

1a *Working in straight lines.*

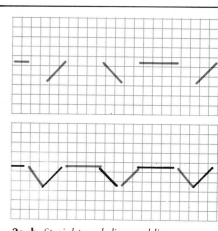

2a, b *Straight and diagonal lines.*

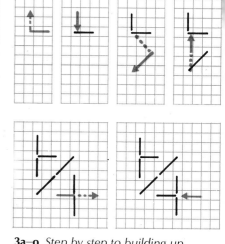

3a–o *Step by step to building up individual units by working in circular movements. This pattern could be worke*

Creating Blackwork patterns

All you need to create your blackwork patterns are graph paper, a ruler and a sharp pointed pencil. Work on the basis of one line on the graph equalling one thread of fabric and draw the patterns using basic geometric shapes from which you can develop intricate and interesting patterns. In order to stitch continuously around the design, so that you do not waste thread, you can work straight lines to form a plain grid or straight lines including diagonals or you can move in continuous circles for complicated patterns.

⊞	*Threads of fabric*
───	*New stitch on right side*
- - - -	*New stitch on wrong side*
⟶	*Direction of stitch*
⟅	*Back stitch*
⬭	*Detached chain stitch*
━━━	*Stitch already worked*

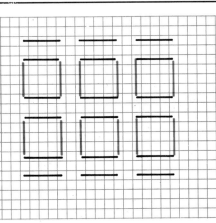

1b *Completing the basic grid.*

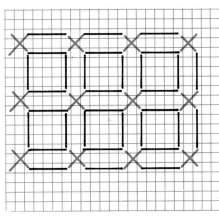

1c *Filling in with cross-stitch.*

1d *The complete pattern.*

2c *Completing the basic grid.*

2d *Starting the inner grid*

2e *The complete pattern*

in lines to form the grid although it would need long stitches on the wrong side, but by stitching complicated patterns in

circular movements you can work more quickly, and use less thread.

The plain pattern (top left) with the design completed by rosettes of detached chain stitch.

53

Fabric required

Evenweave embroidery fabric, 24in square, with 18 threads per 1in.

You will also need

Threads, pearl cotton, one 10grm ball No. 5 and two 10grm balls No. 8 in black, seven spools twisted silk.
Tapestry needles, No. 26 for silk thread and No. 22 for pearl cotton.
Plywood 20in square (this can be larger if you want a wide frame).
Staples and staple gun
Glass and framing materials

The design

1 First check that the fabric is cut on the straight grain or straighten if necessary. Find the center of each side of the fabric by folding it in half and marking the fold at each edge with a few basting stitches. Open out the fabric, refold the other way and mark the fold again.
2 Starting at the center, and 4 inches in from the edge on one side, begin by out-lining the shape of the board in backstitch, using the No. 5 pearl cotton and working each stitch over three threads of the fabric. At 2 inch intervals all the way around on the backstitch border, work a single stitch of the same size at right angles and facing inward to indicate the chart for the squares (if you do this there will be no need to recount the threads). Complete the chart by joining up the single stitches in lines across the board.
3 Work the patterns of your choice, using different threads to give variety. Work the border to the size you desire.

Finishing

Press the embroidery on the wrong side. Stretch over the plywood and secure on the wrong side with staples. Cover with glass and frame.

This town scene, designed by Pauline Liu, is a clever example of how blackwork gives contrasting tone values by varying the density of the stitchery.

RP
1975

One way of keeping a permanent record of blackwork patterns is to work a sampler, such as this one designed as a chess-board by Pamela Tubby.

DRAWN AND PULLED THREAD WORK
Drawn thread work

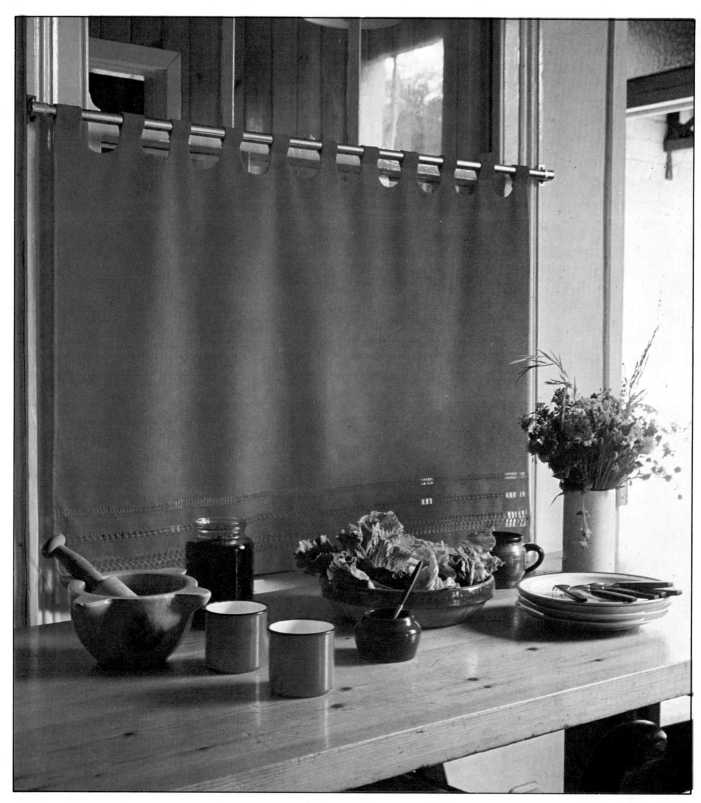

Drawn thread work is a method of embroidery which creates a lacy fabric from a plain, closely woven one. It is primarily used for decorative borders for table linen where threads parallel to the edge of the fabric are withdrawn and the remaining threads in the border (those at right angles to the edge) are grouped together by simple stitchery.

The fabric

When choosing a fabric for drawn thread work the most important considerations are that it should be evenweave (with an equal number of warp and weft threads) which can be easily counted and withdrawn.

Linen is the traditional choice for drawn thread work (perhaps because of its durability for table linen), and it is available in an even-weave with a thread count which varies from very fine to the coarser heavier variety.

There are many other suitable evenweave fabrics, including some synthetics, which do not need ironing and are very practical for place mats, table cloths, etcetera. To decide whether a fabric is evenweave, cut a hole 1 inch square in a piece of cardboard, hold it over the fabric and count the threads enclosed in the "window" – there should be the same number in both directions.

The threads

Threads for this type of embroidery need to be strong and hard wearing. It is usually best to choose a matching thread which is slightly heavier than the threads of the fabric for the decorative stitching and a finer one for hem stitching and buttonholing. On a medium-weight linen, for example, a light weight embroidery thread (not 6-strand) is suitable for hem-stitching and buttonholing, with a slightly heavier one for the additional stitchery. However, it is worth experimenting with the thread on a spare piece of fabric since it might do well and be effective to use one thread throughout.

The needles

Tapestry needles of appropriate size should always be used because their blunt points separate the threads of the fabric while a regular sewing needle might split them.

The stitches

The simplest form of drawn thread work is hem-stitching, in which the outer edge of the border is level with the inner edge of the hem so that the stitching can be

Café curtains given a neat but delicate border by the use of drawn thread work.

worked alternately to secure the hem and group the threads in the border. There are numerous decorative ways in which the threads of the border can be stitched, twisted or knotted together. Some of the most commonly used stitches are ladder stitch, coral knot, double knot and herringbone stitch.

Hem-stitched borders

Before starting a major project, it is advisable to work a simple hem-stitched border for a place mat or napkin.

1 Decide on the finished depth of the hem and measure in double this amount plus the depth of the first turning.

2 Using the point of a tapestry needle, pull out the thread immediately above the total depth of the hem and withdraw it across the width of the fabric.

3 Continue to pull out threads of fabric until the border is the desired depth.

4 Turn up the hem to the edge of the border and baste in place.

5 To work the hem-stitching, first knot the end of the thread and run it along the hem so that the knot is securely inside.

6 Starting at the edge of the fabric, wrap the working thread around the first two threads of the border, make a hem stitch into the fold of the hem as for regular hemming, then overcast the next two threads of the border. Continue in this way, overcasting the threads of the border and hemming the fold alternately for the length of the border, always picking up the same number of threads each time.

7 To strengthen the opposite edge of the border, work along it in a similar way, overcasting the same pairs of threads and

overcasting the edge of the fabric to match the hemmed side.

Four-sided and satin stitch border

When working a border around all four sides of a cloth, the threads are withdrawn in a slightly different way.

1 Calculate the total depth of the hem as for a simple border. Measure in this amount from both directions in each corner and mark the point where they meet with a pin or colored tack to indicate the outer corners of the border. Threads must not be withdrawn beyond this point.

2 Cut the first thread of the border 1 inch away from the marked point at both ends. Pull out the cut ends as far as the point and leave them hanging. Pull out the remaining portion of thread completely from the middle.

3 Continue to withdraw threads in this way all around the border for the required depth.

4 The strongest and neatest way of securing the loose threads at the corners is to turn them back into the hem and enclose them when the hem is stitched. Alternatively, on a very fine and firmly woven linen the threads can be cut close to the edge and secured by buttonhole stitch.

5 Turn up the hem, mitering the corners, and stitch the diagonal fold neatly.

6 Work the hem stitching as for a simple border.

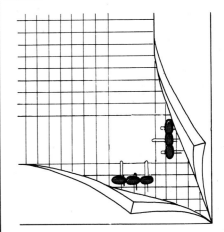

Drawn thread insertions and borders

These insertions can all be used for table linen, to decorate the hems of curtains and, if worked in a heavier thread, for garments. Most drawn thread insertions are first hem stitched along both edges, thus securing the hem if the insertions are used as a border and strengthening the edges when used as plain insertions. They may also be used for tying the threads together for the final decorative stitches.

Twisted border

In this insertion, the tied threads are twisted together into bunches of two or three. For wide insertions, two or three rows of twisting can be worked. Beads can also be picked up on the needle between each twisting to make an attractive variation.

1 Using a heavier or contrasting thread to the one used for hemstitching, anchor it to the middle of the outside edge of the corner square of the border.

2 Pass the needle over the space to form one spoke of the spider's web filling to be completed later.

3 Take the needle over the first two tied groups of threads, then back under the second group and over the first group. Pull

the thread taut so that the groups twist.

4 Repeat this process along the whole border, take the thread across to the opposite side of the corner space and fasten off on the wrong side.

5 Continue in this way on each side of the border.

6 Add four extra crossing threads to the four already formed in each corner space and complete the wheel or web.

Coral stitch twisted border

This is worked in a similar way, but coral stitch is used to tie the groups together.

Lattice border

The groups of threads are drawn together with a binding stitch, by taking the thread alternately above and below the groups.

1 Pass the needle over the first two groups, bring the needle around the second group, pass it over the second and third group, around the third group and over the third and fourth group.

2 Continue in this way, binding the bunches above and below as shown, passing the needle behind the bars from right to left and keeping the working thread above the needle behind the bars from right to left for the lower bars.

Needleweaving border

This can be very effective when worked on a heavy slubbed linen with a combination of self and contrasting threads.

1 Work the hem-stitching along each edge, tying the threads into bunches of four.

2 Run the working threads into the hem or edge above the starting point, leaving about 1 inch to be darned in when the needle weaving is finished.

3 Bring the needle through the hem or edge and pass it over the first four threads to the right, bring the needle up again at the starting point and pass it over and under the first two threads to the left.

4 Working on these four threads, weave over and under until you are halfway down the block of withdrawn threads.

5 Pass the needle to the next four threads to the right and continue weaving over this block until you reach the opposite edge of the insertion.

6 Carry the working thread inside this completed block of weaving until you reach the starting point of the block in the middle of the border.

7 Start weaving upward on the next group of four threads to the right, continuing to the top of the border.

8 Continue to weave upward and downward on the groups, carrying the needle through the woven blocks to the next position.

9 When you reach the end of the insertion, return to the beginning and weave on the remaining threads in each block to complete the insertion. Fasten the thread securely and thread it back through the last block of weaving to make the work neat. The weaving should be as neat on the back as on the front of the work.

Finishing the corners

Where the withdrawn threads meet at the corners of a border a small square space is formed which should be strengthened and filled with stitchery, such as a woven spider's web. This should be worked after the hem stitching and additional stitchery is worked.

Pulled thread work

Pulled thread work is a method of creating a pattern of holes, spaces or shapes on an even-weave fabric with embroidery stitches which are pulled tightly.

This type of embroidery is ideal for making all kinds of table linen and for lampshades, borders on garments, curtains, bedspreads and pillows.

Sometimes known as drawn fabric work, it is of European peasant origin and started with the use of embroidery on loosely woven muslins and calicos. To prevent the threads from lying loosely over the fabric the stitches were pulled tightly and it was discovered that this could create attractive patterns.

Pulled thread work should not be confused with drawn thread work, in which the pattern is created by actually withdrawing threads from the fabric and stitching on those remaining.

The fabric

Pulled thread work is a form of counted thread embroidery where the stitches are worked over a specific number of threads. For this reason the fabric should be of an even-weave (one with an equal number of warp and weft threads to the same measurement) and the threads should be large enough to count easily.

Several kinds of fabric are suitable, such as linen in various weights, from heavy home furnishing linen to linen scrim used for cleaning; cotton in many weights and colors; evenweave wools; Moygashel dress fabrics and synthetic home furnishing fabrics.

The thread

Generally the thread used for the stitchery should be of equal thickness to a withdrawn thread of the fabric, with the addition of thicker or thinner threads to vary the texture and pattern. If the fabric is a good one and will unravel easily, it is possible to remove threads from an unused end and work the embroidery in these.

Other suitable threads include the pearl and crochet cottons which are available in all weights and in a good range of colors, and although traditionally this type of embroidery was worked in self-color thread, today a contrast color is often used.

Pure silk buttonhole thread is good too, particularly when a fine thread of silky texture is needed. Threads to avoid are stranded embroidery floss, linen threads and mercerized sewing cotton, since these tend to fray and break.

Needles

Always use a tapestry needle for pulled thread work as this will not split the threads of the fabric. Normally the needle should be of a suitable weight for the fabric so it passes between the threads easily. But when you are working a border or edging in a progressive stitch such as three-sided or four-sided stitch, you may find it easier to use a larger needle than that used for the rest of the work.

Frames

Always use a frame for this type of work as it will keep it at an even tension, prevent the fabric from pulling out of shape and enable the threads to be counted easily. The only exception to this rule would be when you are working an edging.

The stitches

The stitches used in pulled thread embroidery are some of the easiest to work and many are based on satin stitch, worked in lines or blocks either at an even tension or pulled tightly. When these two methods are combined, a pattern is produced which can be varied at will. A combination of only two stitches, such as four-sided stitch and satin stitch, can produce a number of patterns when the tension and stitch order are varied. Honeycomb stitch and three-sided stitch are other stitches used. (Border stitches are covered in the next chapter.)

Before you start a project, it is advisable to practice some of the stitches, working each separately and then in combinations, using both thin and thick threads (such as a fine crochet cotton and a heavier pearl cotton).

To begin stitching do not use a knot but bring the thread through the fabric some distance away from the stitching point and make a small backstitch to anchor it. Continue working until the thread is finished then return to the starting point and darn in the surplus thread through the stitching line. Alternatively, hold the end of the thread under the stitching line for a short way and work over it.

To finish stitching darn in the end of the thread to the stitchery on the back of the work, making a small backstitch to secure it. Pulled thread work should be as neat on the back of the fabric as on the front, particularly for table linen and lampshades.

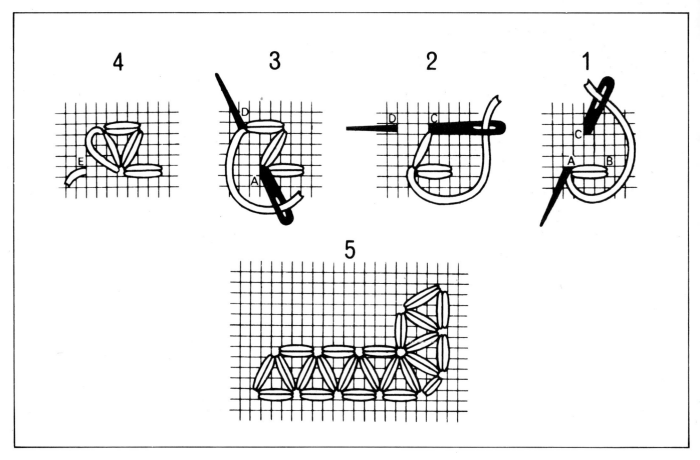

Three-sided stitch (A)

This stitch is worked from right to left. Figure 1: Bring the thread through at A and make two stitches from A to B over four threads of fabric. Bring the needle through at A and take two stitches to C. Figure 2. Bring the needle through at D and take two stitches from D to C. Figure 3. Take two stitches from D to A. Figure 4. Bring the needle through at E. Figure 5. Turning a corner.

Honeycomb filling stitch (B)

This stitch is worked from the top down. Figure 1. Bring the needle through at the arrow and insert at A. Bring through at B and insert at A. Bring through at B and insert at C. Bring through at D, insert again at C and bring through at D. Continue in this way for the row. Figure 2. Where rows connect, the vertical stitches are worked into the same holes.

Four-sided stitch (C)

This stitch is worked from right to left. Figure 1: Bring the thread through at the arrow, insert it at A and bring it through at B. Figure 2: Insert at the arrow and bring it out at D.
Figure 3: Insert at A and bring it out at B. Continue in this way for a row or close the end for a single stitch.

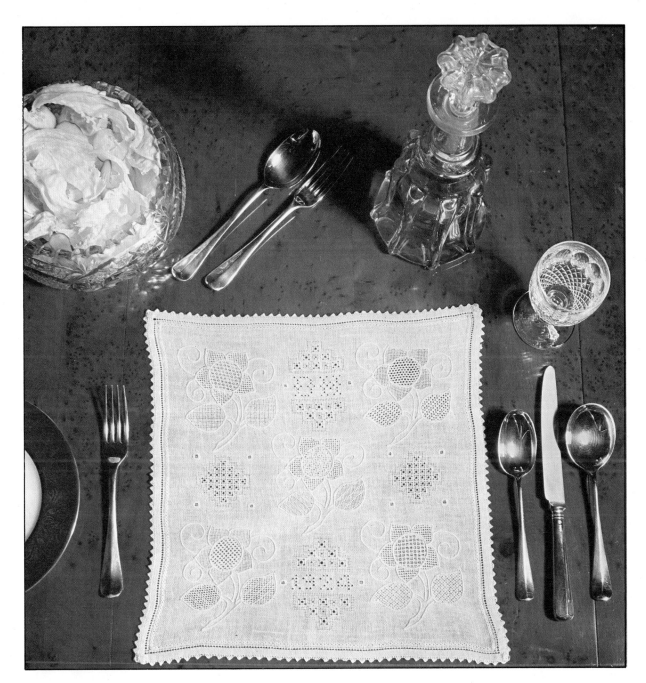

Edgings and borders

One of the most attractive of the various techniques of pulled thread work is to combine them to form simple yet decorative borders on all types of household linen.

Four sided borders

This border is suitable for table linen or to decorate the panels of a lampshade. It combines a repeating pattern of seven satin stitches worked over eight threads with a block of four four-sided stitches worked over four threads. The satin stitch is pulled tightly and the four-sided stitch is worked at normal tension.

1 Using a thread similar in weight to the fabric, work seven satin stitches over eight threads of the fabric. Follow this by four four-sided stitches worked over the center four threads of the eight. Continue in this way to the end of the row.

2 Repeat this row two or three times to form a border of the desired width (you will normally need a wider border for a lampshade than for a place mat, for example).

3 Start the next row with four four-sided stitches worked over the center four threads of a block of eight. Continue with seven satin stitches over all the eight threads. Continue in this way to the end of the row.

4 Repeat this row until you have the same number of rows as the first pattern. The satin stitches should alternate with the four-sided stitches every two or three rows, depending on the width of the pattern desired. The pattern can be varied further by changing the stitch sequence in alternate rows.

Honeycomb and satin stitch border

This border can be worked vertically as shown in the previous chapter to decorate the panels of a lampshade, or it can be worked horizontally for table linen. Follow the diagram for honeycomb stitch, but incorporate eight satin stitches pulled tightly, followed by one backstitch and eight more satin stitches from each backstitch section of honeycomb stitch.

1 Bring the needle through at the arrow.
2 Insert the needle four threads to the right.
3 Bring the needle through four threads down at B.
4 Insert the needle again at A and bring through two threads below.
5 Work eight satin stitches pulled tightly over these two threads.
6 Work one backstitch pulled tightly over four threads and bring the needle through two threads below the first row of satin stitches.
7 Work eight satin stitches pulled tightly below the first row.
8 Proceed to the next honeycomb stitch and repeat as before.
9 When the line of stitching is the desired length, turn the work and repeat the honeycomb and satin stitch combination until the border is complete.

Incorporating beads into the work

The honeycomb and satin stitch border can be made more decorative by adding perhaps a pearl bead of the right size in the center space which is formed between the two rows of honeycomb stitching. Use a strong thread to secure the bead with two stitches before passing on to the next space. Carry the thread from space to space along the back of the work and finish off with a secure overcasting stitch on the back of the work.

Eyelets

These are also simple to work and effective, either singly or in groups. They consist of a number of straight stitches worked into a central hole, usually over a square of eight threads of fabric. They can be arranged in groups to form a pattern, or worked singly as squares or rectangles. Some of the most popular are square eyelet, single cross eyelet and back-stitched eyelet. These can all be worked as rectangles as well as squares, and they can also be grouped irregularly together, leaving part of the eyelet unworked.

Square eyelet

This is worked over a square of eight threads.
1 Begin in the center of one side and take a straight stitch over four threads and into the center hole.
2 Bring the needle up in the next space to the right and take a straight stitch over four threads and into the center hole. Continue in this way around the square until the eyelet is complete.

Single cross eyelet

Work in a similar way over eight threads

as for the square eyelet, but leave one thread free between each quarter.

Backstitched eyelet

This is also worked over eight threads.
1 Begin in the center of one side and work one straight stitch over four threads and into the center hole.
2 Bring the needle out two threads beyond the straight stitch and make a backstitch into it, then work one straight stitch over four threads and into the center hole. Continue around the sides of the square until the eyelet is completed.

Pulled fabric edgings

One of the features of pulled thread embroidery is that it can be worked around the edge of the fabric and incorporated into the hem. The three following edgings are all suitable for most types of table linen.

Edging 1

This is a very simple edging and consists of two rows of four-sided stitch, one of which is worked through a fold or double thickness of fabric.
1 On the right side of the fabric count 10 or 12 threads up from the raw edge and work one row of four-sided stitch over four threads for the desired distance.
2 Fold the fabric to the wrong side so that the fold is level with the outer edge of the stitching. Baste in place.
3 On the right side of the fabric work the second row of four-sided stitch through the double thickness of fabric.
4 Remove the basting and trim the surplus

edge back to the line of stitching.

Edging 2

This is worked in the same way as the first edging with the addition of two rows of buttonhole stitch. Work the buttonhole stitch with a fine and firmly twisted thread to produce a hard-wearing edging and use a slightly larger tapestry needle than usual for the four-sided stitch so that the buttonhole stitch will be easier to work.
1 Count 10 or 12 threads in from the raw edge and work a row of four-sided stitch over four threads as before.
2 Turn the raw edge onto the wrong side and work the second row of four-sided stitch through the double fabric.

3 Using a small tapestry needle, on the right side of the fabric and over the folded edge, work five buttonhole stitches into each hole made by the first row of four-sided stitch.
4 Work a second row of buttonhole stitch into the holes formed by the second row of four-sided stitch.
5 For a deeper border, more rows of four-sided stitch can be worked. The edging will be further defined if you work the

buttonholing in a darker thread.

Edging 3

1 Count 10 threads in from the raw edge of the fabric and fold the fabric over to the wrong side along this thread. Baste in place.
2 Count three threads in from the fold and work a row of three-sided stitch over the next four threads on the right side of the fabric.
3 Work one row of four-sided stitch above the three-sided stitch.
4 Cut the surplus fabric back to the second line of stitching.
5 Work five buttonhole stitches into each stitch hole formed by the four-sided stitch.
6 To finish the edging, work five buttonhole stitches over the three threads along the folded edge and into the holes formed by the three-sided stitch.

Turning corners

To turn a corner using four-sided stitch, count the threads and check that the number is divisible by four.
To turn a corner using three-sided stitch, count the threads as you near the corner and adjust the fold of the hem so that the stitch can be worked over four threads across the corner.
The corner can also be turned by working one-third of three-sided stitch, known as eyelet filling stitch. The base of the three-sided stitch used for this should come across the corner to be turned.

Pulled fabric runner

This elegant drawn fabric table runner will fit in with any decor, traditional or modern. The three stitches used, satin stitch, ringed backstitch and honeycomb filling are simple to work. Make the runner longer or shorter if you wish, to fit your own furniture.

Size
35 inches by 12 inches

Fabric required
$\frac{5}{8}$yd off-white evenweave fabric, 21 threads to 1in, 59 in wide.
D.M.C. 6-strand Floss, 15 skeins 420 snuff brown.
Tapestry needle No. 20.

The design
1 Cut a piece from the fabric measuring 13½ inches by 37½ inches. Mark the center of the fabric lengthwise with a line of stitches. This acts as a guide when placing the design. The working chart shows a section of the design, with the center marked by a blank arrow which should coincide with the line of basting stitches.
2 Each stitch must be pulled firmly, except the satin stitch triangles which are worked with normal tension.
3 Use six strands of thread for satin stitch and three strands for the rest of the embroidery.
4 With the long side of the fabric facing, begin working the design with ringed backstitch, 1¾ in from the narrow edge of the fabric. Continue until the embroidery measures 34 inches. Work the rest of the embroidery outward from this central band. Repeat the three outer lines of satin stitch 3 inches from the central band of embroidery.

Ringed backstitch
This stitch is worked from right to left and can be used as a border or as a filling. It is worked in two steps as shown in the diagrams. Figure 1: bring the thread through at the arrow; insert the needle at A (2 threads down), bring it through at B (4 threads up and 2 threads to the left); insert at arrow, bring it through at C (2 threads up and 4 threads to the left); insert the needle at B, bring it through at D (2 threads down and 4 to the left); insert it at C, bring it through at E (4 threads down and 2 to the left). Continue making half rings of backstitch for the required length. Figure 2: turn the fabric around

Mitring the corners

The chart shows a section of the design, indicating the position of the stitches.

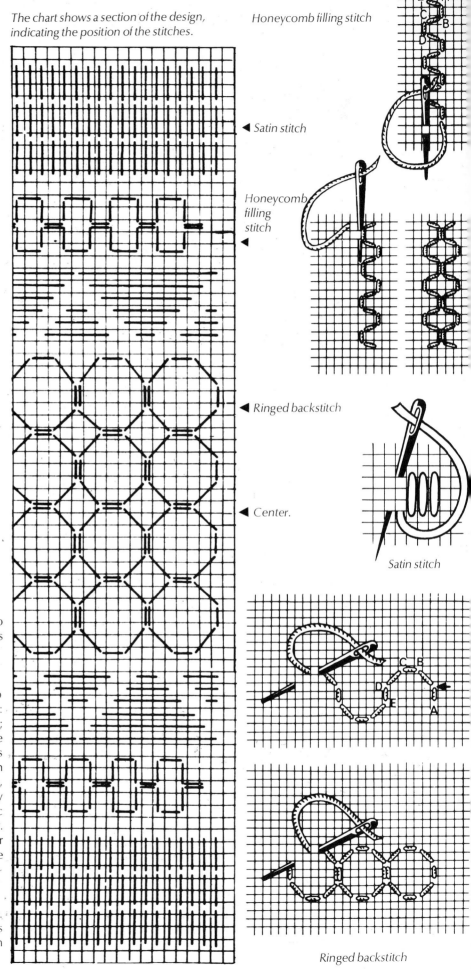

◄ Satin stitch

Honeycomb
filling
stitch ◄

◄ Ringed backstitch

◄ Center.

Honeycomb filling stitch

Satin stitch

Ringed backstitch

and work back in the same way to complete the rings. All connecting stitches are worked in the same holes.

Honeycomb filling stitch

This stitch is worked from the top downward again in two stages. Figure 1: bring the thread through at the arrow; insert the needle at A (2 threads to the right), bring it through at B (2 threads down); insert again at A, bring through at B; insert at C (2 threads to the left), bring through at D. Continue in this way for the desired length. Turn the fabric around and work back in the same way. Figure 2 shows the work turned ready for the second row. Figure 3 shows the completed stitch. Pull each stitch firmly.

Finishing

Press the embroidery on the wrong side. Turn back ½ inch hems. Miter the corners and slip stitch. Press the runner again on the wrong side.

HARDANGER WORK

Hardanger work, sometimes called Norwegian embroidery, originated in a district by the same name in western Norway where the local inhabitants were famous for their fine work.

It is a form of drawn thread work which is quick and easy. Geometric in design with an overall heavy openwork appearance, it is very popular in Scandinavia where it is used for adorning traditional dress and household linens.

The main characteristic of this type of embroidery is the rectangular grouping of satin stitch, known as kloster blocks, arranged to outline the spaces and build up the basic portion of the design.

Fabric and threads

Hardanger embroidery requires a fabric with a very regular weave in which the warp and weft threads are equal, or special Hardanger linen or canvas which is woven with double warp and weft threads so that it is extremely strong and does not fray in cutting.

This embroidery is traditionally worked on white or natural linen with self-colored threads although the work can be very effective if a dark thread is used on a light ground or vice versa.

The working threads should be slightly coarser than the threads of the fabric for the satin stitch blocks which form the basis of the design, and slightly finer for the fillings of the open work spaces. Coton à broder and pearl cotton are most suitable for more traditional work.

However, provided the fabrics are of suitable weight and even weave, you can break with tradition and use synthetic or wool fabrics and threads to create your own exciting and contemporary designs for wall hangings, lampshades, pillow covers, dress insertions and accessories. The only tools required are tapestry needles and a pair of very sharp pointed embroidery scissors.

The design

By its very nature the design has to be geometrical in form, with square, triangle, diamond or oblong shapes.

The main outlines of the design should be kept as simple as possible and the basic shapes and their relationship to each other in forming a pattern can easily be worked out on graph paper. The design can be developed by building up small shapes around and within the larger shapes, and adding surface stitchery.

Working the design

It is essential throughout the work that both the threads and stitches are counted with great accuracy and that the fabric is carefully cut because any irregularity would spoil the general effect. If a frame is used, it is much easier to achieve this and to keep the embroidery at an even tension.

There are four steps in working Hardanger embroidery.

1 Outlining the spaces and design with kloster blocks.

2 Working any surface embroidery.

3 Cutting and drawing the threads for the open spaces.

4 Decorating the bars of the larger spaces and adding the lace stitch fillings.

Kloster blocks

A kloster block is made up of an irregular number of stitches enclosing a regular number of fabric threads. Five stitches to a block is the usual size, but this can vary from nine stitches enclosing eight threads to three stitches enclosing two. The blocks may be grouped vertically or horizontally to outline the space.

To make a vertical line across the fabric to outline a diamond or triangle the blocks should be worked in steps following the weave of the fabric. If you wish to accentuate certain shapes the blocks may be varied in height as well as length. The head of the stitch should always face the cut space to protect the ends of the fabric and to prevent them from fraying.

Surface stitchery

In addition to the outlining blocks, decorative surface stitchery is added to create interest and to enrich the design. This should correspond to the general pattern and principle of following the weave of fabric and a variety of stitches can be used, such as backstitch, star-stitch, herringbone, eyelets, backstitched or woven wheels, four-sided and interlacing stitches.

Cutting the threads

In Hardanger work the embroidery is half complete before the work is cut, unlike other drawn thread work where the threads are removed first and then the decorative stitchery applied.

Using very sharp scissors, cut the threads in the spaces enclosed by the blocks close to the stitches. Complete one motif at a time, removing either all the horizontal threads or the vertical threads, but not both at the same time.

When the cutting is complete it will have created an open mesh of geometric patterns within the outline of the blocks. These now need to be strengthened and decorated.

Decorating the bars

The bars of the threads left in the spaces can be strengthened by overcasting or needleweaving, although it is advisable not to mix the two methods.

At this stage decide whether you want to incorporate lace stitch fillings to add to the delicacy of the work since these are made as a series of twists or loops while the bars are being covered.

On articles not subject to wear, you could leave the bars without weaving or overcasting and just add a filling or interlocking lace stitch. An attractive filling for a larger space can be a backstitched or woven wheel, worked over an even number of anchoring threads.

1 Work the overcasting diagonally across a group of threads, making each stitch firm and covering each bar completely. When one bar is done, carry the thread behind the work to the next bar, leaving a small square of fabric visible between the bars at the intersections.

2 Work the needleweaving over the bars, following the method given in the section on pulled thread work. At this stage if you are not adding a lace stitch filling, you could incorporate small picots.

3 If you do this, place the picots on each side of the bar in the middle, twisting the thread around the needle to make the picot on one side and then moving to the other side and repeating the process.

Hardanger work table cloth

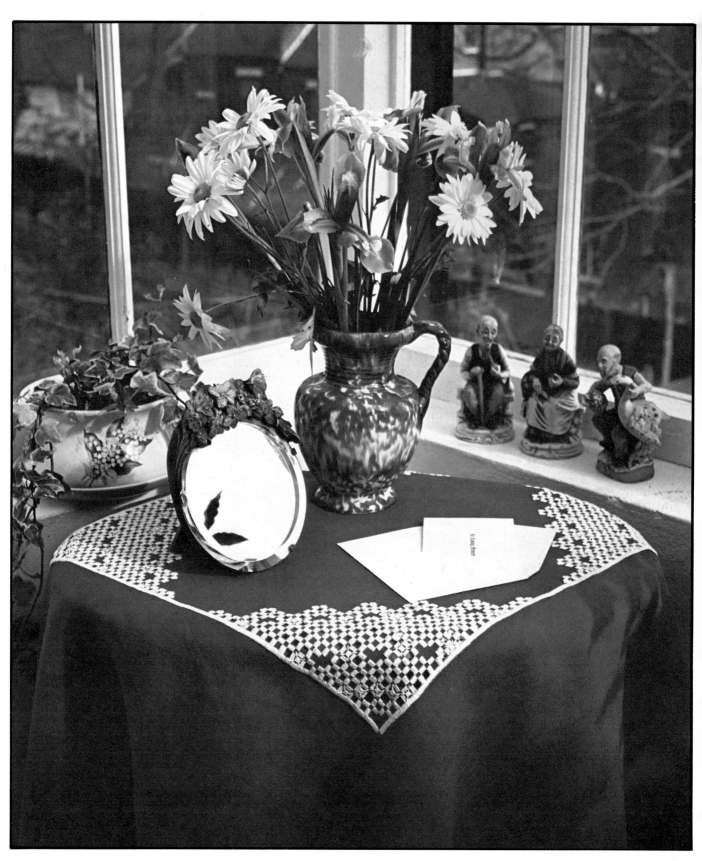

Size
50 inches square

Fabric required
1½ yds of 52 in wide medium weight Hardanger linen with 29 threads to 1 in.

You will also need
D.M.C. Pearl cotton No. 5, 3 × 10 grm balls: white.
D.M.C. Pearl cotton No. 8, 1 × 10 grm balls: white.
Tapestry needles, 1 each No. 20 and No. 24.

Preparing the fabric
Trim the fabric so that it is an exact square. Mark the center in both directions with lines of basting.

The design
This tablecloth uses the techniques of Hardanger embroidery, described in the previous chapter. The layout diagram shows the placing of the design for one quarter of the cloth and this is repeated on the remaining three-quarters. The broken lines correspond to the basted lines across the center of the fabric, the numerals indicate the number of threads, and the shaded area is the section given in figure 1. Figure 1 shows the stitches in a section of the design and how they are arranged on the threads. Follow figure 1 and the number key for the actual embroidery, and the layout diagram for the placing of the design. Work all parts similar to the numbered parts in the same stitch.

Working the embroidery
1 Using the No. 5 Pearl cotton and the

LAYOUT DIAGRAM

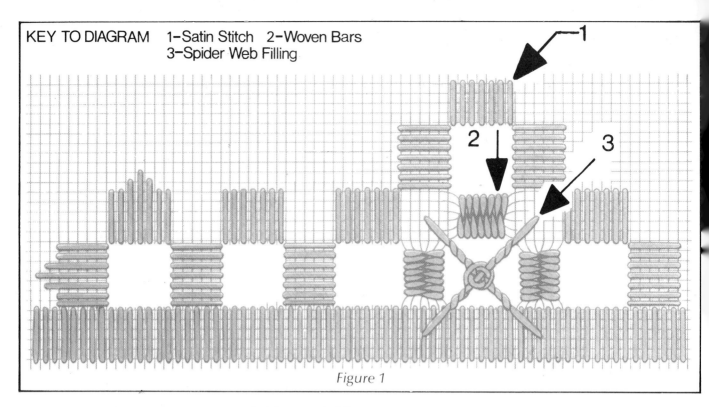

KEY TO DIAGRAM   1-Satin Stitch   2-Woven Bars
                  3-Spider Web Filling

Figure 1

No. 20 tapestry needle, start the embroidery at the black arrow 1 shown in the layout diagram, 266 threads down from the crossed basting threads. Work this part as shown.

2 When all the satin stitch blocks are complete, cut away the threads shown in the black squares on the layout diagram and blank on figure 1.

3 Using the No. 8 Pearl cotton and No. 24 tapestry needle, work the woven bars and fillings (see below) and then complete the remaining sections of the cloth in the same way.

Woven bars
Withdraw an even number of threads from the areas shown in figure 1 and separate the remaining threads into bars with three threads in each by weaving over and under them until the threads are completely covered.

Spider's web filling
1 Work one twisted bar by carrying the thread diagonally across the space. Enter the fabric as shown, twist that thread over the first thread and return to the starting point.

2 Work another twisted bar in the opposite direction but twist the thread back to the center only.

3 Pass the thread over and under the crossed bars twice and then under and over twice. Complete the twisting of the second bar.

Finishing
Press the embroidery on the wrong side. Make 1 inch hems all around, mitering the corners.

NEEDLEWEAVING

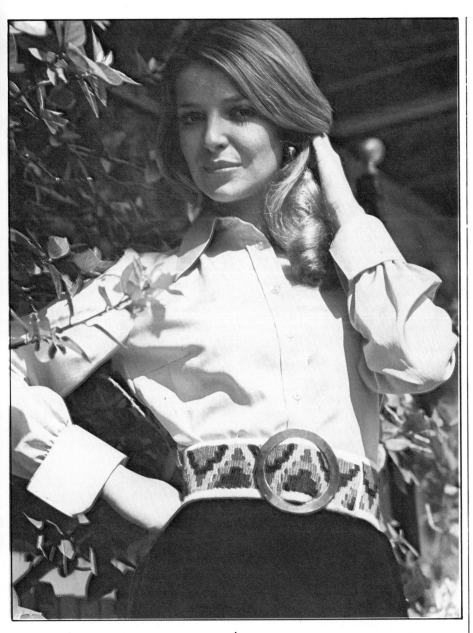

Needleweaving is an ancient craft dating back three thousand years. Most of the early examples are Coptic, and they are known today as loom embroideries since it is thought they were incorporated into the main weaving process of the fabric. Needleweaving is a form of drawn thread work and consists of a decorative pattern worked in weaving or darning stitch upon warp or weft threads after some of the crosswise threads have been withdrawn.

The fabric

Needleweaving is usually worked on a foundation of evenly woven fabric from which threads can be easily removed. Burlap, heavy linen, cottons, woolens and tweed, as well as some acrylic curtain fabrics, are all suitable.

The threads

The choice of threads is limitless provided that they are of a similar weight or slightly heavier than the withdrawn threads of the fabric. If the threads supporting the weaving are sufficiently open and strong, you can incorporate a variety of threads, such as carpet yarn, chenille, straw, heavy nub yarn and even string, leather thongs, ribbon and thin strips of nylon. Beads, rings and metal washers can all be added as the weaving progresses to add interest and texture.

Needles

You will need an assortment of heavy tapestry needles in the right sizes to take the threads you are using. If you are planning to incorporate fine ribbon or thongs, an elastic threader or large, blunt-ended needle is useful.

The design

If you want a fairly free design, the simplest way is to choose a fabric and some interesting threads, and begin work without spending time working out the design first — some of the most exciting results with needleweaving can be created spontaneously.

If the needleweaving is worked for a specific purpose, such as a border with a geometric pattern or in the form of a repeating pattern arranged symmetrically to fill a given space, you should first chart the design on graph paper, showing how the motifs are linked and which colors are to be used.

Preparing the fabric

If the needleweaving is for a border, prepare the fabric by withdrawing the threads in the same way as for drawn thread work. If you are weaving a simple repeating pattern, however, it would be helpful to hem stitch the threads into even groups of threads at the top and bottom of the border as this helps you count the threads during the weaving process. If you are working on a heavy, loosely woven fabric in which the threads are easily counted, this step is not necessary.

The stitch

Weaving or darning stitch is worked by passing the needle over one thread, under the next and so on. If you prefer, you can divide the threads into blocks of two, three or four and pass the needle over and under each block.

To start weaving, insert the needle about an inch above the first block of weaving and pull it through, leaving a length of thread to be darned in later. Begin weaving between the first and second group of threads, working from left to right. Continue weaving between the threads for the desired amount, making sure that each row of stitches lies close to the preceding one and is not pulled too tightly.

To pass to the next block of threads, slip your needle up the side of the block to the top and then work over the next block. You can also pass from one block of weaving to the next by darning the working thread through the back of the work.

If you are using several different types of thread, take care to maintain an even tension.

More open effects

You can vary the solid effect of needleweaving with single bars of overcasting with satin stitch. Work needleweaving over the first blocks of threads for four or six rows then return to the beginning of the block and overcast the first two threads with satin stitch. Slip the needle up the side of the overcast threads and start to weave over the next block. If you wish, the overcast bars can be woven over in the middle of the border.

Needlewoven belt

This belt can be made in wool as shown in the photograph or you can make it in an evenweave cotton or linen, using soft embroidery or pearl cotton.

Size

3 inches wide, to fit any waist size

Fabric required

$\frac{1}{4}$ yd fabric × the length of belt required + 2 in (for buckle), with approximately 14 threads to 1 in.

You will also need

D.M.C. Tapestry Yarn: 4 skeins black; 3 skeins each chestnut 7174, 7176; 1 skein in chestnut 7178.
3 inches × the length of belt of non-woven interfacing.
Buckle.
Tapestry needle No. 18.

The design

The design is a repeating pattern which can be adjusted to make a belt to your own measurements. The diagram below gives a part of the design with the colors used for each area.

Preparing the fabric

With one long side of the fabric facing you, withdraw 26 lengthwise threads through the center 2 inches in from each end. Darn in the ends neatly.

Working the needleweaving

1 With one long side facing, start the needleweaving at the left-hand edge and work the section given following diagram 1 and the letter key for the colors. Diagram 2 shows how the needleweaving is worked over four threads of fabric and how the connecting stitch is worked over and under the start of a new block.
2 Repeat the section until all the loose threads are woven.

Finishing the belt

1 Trim the fabric to within $2\frac{1}{2}$ inches on the long sides of the belt and to within $\frac{3}{4}$ inch on the short ends.
2 Sew the interfacing lightly in place along the center on the wrong side of the work.
3 Fold one long side of fabric over the interfacing and baste. Turn under the seam allowance of $\frac{1}{2}$ inch on the other side and hem in place along the center of the wrong side of the belt. Turn under the seam allowance at each short end and sew in place. Sew the buckle to one short end of the belt.

7174   7176   7178   black

CUT WORK
Simple techniques

Cut work is the name given to open-work types of embroidery where portions of the background are cut away and in the more elaborate forms, re-embroidered. Cut work is basically the link between embroidery and needlemade lace and should not be confused with Hardanger and Hedebo, the counted thread methods.

Types of cut work
There are four main types of cut work, varying from simple cut spaces to larger and more elaborately filled spaces.
In simple cut work (see below), the cut spaces are quite small. In Renaissance work they grow larger, while in Richelieu work the addition of bars and picots gives a more decorative appearance. Venetian work has the largest cut spaces with intricate fillings, giving a lace-like quality to the embroidery. These more elaborate and highly decorative methods are covered in later chapters.

Uses of cut work
Cut work is suitable for all types of household linen and can also be successfully used as dress decoration, provided the design is planned as an integral part of the dress and is not just added as an afterthought.

Fabric and threads
As the main interest of cut work lies in the variation of texture produced by the cut spaces – either as open shapes or decorated with bars, picots, spider's web or woven wheels and needlepoint fillings – color is of secondary importance. Most of the charm of cut work lies in it being self-colored although graded shades of color with simple cut work can be effective. It is important to avoid color contrasts with the more elaborate forms.
Only a firm, evenly woven linen or very strong cotton should be used for cut work because other fabrics fray when the spaces are cut. Choose a linen thread or fine pearl floss or coton à broder in a weight to suit the fabric. Linen lace thread

may also be used, although this is available in cream shades only. Do not use stranded floss because the strands of this thread are not strong enough when divided and would not withstand friction through wear and laundering.

Needles
Fine crewel needles are suitable for simple cut work although sharps are normally best for working the lace-like fillings of the other forms of cut work. Choose the size according to the weight of the thread being used. You may also need tapestry needles in various sizes to work the hems and finish the edges.
You should also have a pair of very sharp, finely pointed embroidery scissors.

Designs for cut work
Traditional cut work designs are nearly always floral and the more intricate fillings of Venetian work are similar to old lace patterns.
Simple cut work has no bars or picots and consists solely of a design of simple shapes worked in buttonhole stitch with the background area around the motif cut away, thus throwing the main part of the design into relief.
All cut work, however elaborate, may be designed initially by arranging cut paper shapes, either as a repetitive border or as a single motif or design, to fit a given size. Whatever the function, the pattern of the cut shapes should balance with the more solid parts of the design.
When planning or adapting a design, check that all the shapes tie up at vital points of the structure, else they will hang loosely when the background is cut away. Draw all the main outlines of the design in double lines to act as a guide for the running stitch which is worked within them to act as padding for the buttonhole stitch. A design of curved or circular shapes is much easier to work in this method than a geometric design with sharp angles.
When your design has been prepared,

transfer it to the fabric using dressmaker's carbon or the prick and pounce method (see the chapter on transferring designs).

The stitches
1 Start by working several rows of running stitch around the motifs inside the double lines. These form a foundation for the buttonholing and enable a firm edge to be worked. The running stitches should lie very evenly on the fabric for if they are pulled too tightly the work will pucker.
2 Work the buttonholing close together with the looped edge of the stitches facing the space which is to be cut away.

3 Using very sharp scissors, cut away the fabric close to the buttonholing. Cut cleanly, using the points of the scissors so that the edge will not fluff.
Do not be tempted to cut away part of the work before all the stitching is completed or the work will pull out of shape.

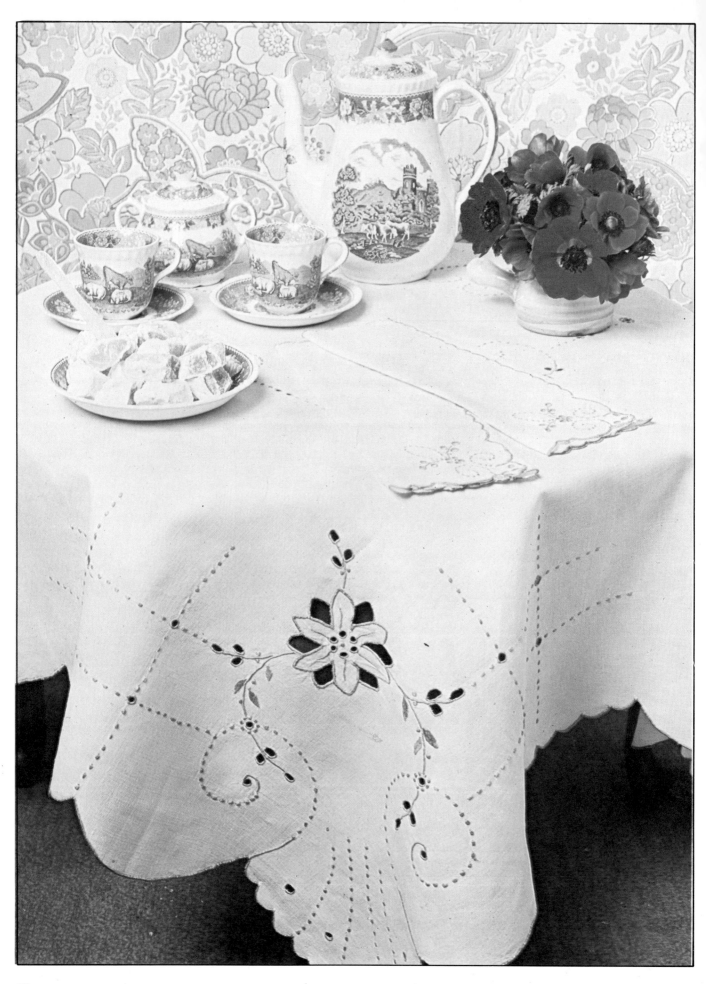

Renaissance and Richelieu cut work

Renaissance and Richelieu cut work are more complicated than simple cut work because the cut spaces are larger and need the addition of bars across the spaces to strengthen and hold together the main parts of the design.

The design

As the bars are the most decorative feature of Renaissance cut work, it is important to place them symmetrically. Where there are larger cut spaces than can be filled adequately with a single straight bar, the bar may be branched. These branched bars show to best advantage if they balance the solid parts of the work, although the cut spaces should not be too large and clumsy. Where a number of bars intersect they can be further enriched by a spider's web or woven wheel filling or by a buttonhole ring.

Fabric and threads

Use the same kinds of fabric and thread as for simple cut work and prepare the embroidery in a similar way.

Working the embroidery

1 When the design has been traced or painted onto the fabric, start the embroidery by working an outer row of padding running stitches. When you reach the position of the first bar, take the thread across the space and make a tiny running stitch within the double lines on that side.

Return the thread to the starting point of

the bar and take another small stitch; then go across the space again.

2 Cover the three threads of the bar with close buttonholing, keeping the bar firm and taking care not to let the needle penetrate the fabric below.

3 Continue with the running stitches around the design until you reach the next bar and work that one in the same way. When all the bars have been worked, complete the second row of padding running stitch.

4 Finish the piece by working close buttonholing over the padding as for simple cut work. Take care not to cut the bars when cutting away the background fabric.

Branched bars

1 Carry the threads across the space in the same way as for a single bar.

2 Work buttonholing over the threads to the point where the bar branches. From this point work the second bar, laying three threads across the space to the point where it joins the double lines. Work the buttonholing over the threads of the second bar back to where it branched from the first bar and then continue working the remaining part of the first bar.

A three or four-branch bar is worked in the same way.

Spider's web filling

If you are filling a large cut space which needs more than a few branched bars, a spider's web filling is a good choice. This filling can be placed in the center or deliberately off-center by altering the angle at which the twists are made.

1 Carry a single thread across the design from top to bottom, then take a tiny stitch between the double lines and take the thread back to the center of the space, twisting the thread around the needle.

2 From the center, take another thread across to the side, twist back to the center and continue in this way, until you have divided the piece into five sections. Before completing the final twist over the last half of the first thread worked, work a woven wheel or spider's web by weaving under and over the five threads. Keep the web or wheel fairly small so that it does not detract from the twisted spokes.

Back-stitched wheel

If the space is large enough, six twists can be worked across it, either at regular or irregular intervals, and then a back-stitched wheel worked over them to complete the design.

Buttonhole ring

This is another decorative filling for a larger cut shape.

1 Wind a fine thread five or six times around a small pencil. Slip the ring off the

pencil, baste it and cover it closely a around with buttonholing.

2 Break off the thread and pin the ring i position on the fabric. To secure the rin to the space, work four or five twisted bar at intervals from the ring to the doubl lines of the design. To carry the thread t the next twist, work a few running stitche along the double lines to avoid spoiling th ring itself.

Richelieu cut work

This is similar to Renaissance cut wor although the cut spaces are a little large and the bars are decorated with picots.

Looped picots. Work the buttonholing over the bar to the center from left t right. Insert a pin into the fabric beneath the bar and pass the working thread unde the head of the pin from left to right, the up over the bar and out under the bar t the right of the pin. Pass the needle through the loop on the pin and the threa beyond it. Pull the working thread tightl to make the picot and continue button-holing to the end of the bar.

Bullion picots. These are worked on the same principle although they are a little more elaborate. Work close buttonholing to the center of the bar, make a bullion stitch from the looped edge of the last stitch by twisting the thread four or five times around the needle and pulling the thread through the twists to make a firm twisted loop. To secure the picot work the next buttonhole stitch close to the previous stitch.

Reticella cut work

This is the most elaborate and lacy form of cut work and bears a strong resemblance to Venetian lace. The types of fabric and working threads are the same as for the other forms of cut work covered in earlier chapters.

The design

The main part of the design for reticella cut work is formed by the stitches worked within the cut squares or geometric shapes. The various fillings are based on a buttonholing or weaving stitch.

While few people today have the time to make large pieces of reticella cut work, small motifs can be made and used to decorate table linens and different kinds of clothing. These motifs are very effective although they do not require the heavy surface stitchery which traditional, examples often contained. A modern pattern or design can be built up by arranging a series of small squares, each containing a

different filling. The squares can be cut out completely, or some threads can be left as a base on which to work the filling stitches.

Preparing the squares

1 Start by marking the position of the squares accurately and outlining them with several rows of running stitch to strengthen the cut area. If you are planning to leave threads within the square, count them and check that there is an even number. Leave the threads in pairs both horizontally and vertically. It often helps to tack a piece of firm white paper behind the squares to give a firmer foundation than the fabric alone, although the stitches are not made into the paper.
2 Cut any threads that are to be removed to within three threads of the running stitch. On firm fine fabrics, turn the cut edges to the back of the work. Overcast the edges and cut away the surplus. On heavier fabrics, work buttonholing over the edge to prevent the filling stitches from pulling away.

Filling open squares

The fillings in an open square are used to build up small solid shapes such as triangles, arcs and semi-circles within a framework of bars worked in buttonholing.
1 Start at the widest part of the design and take a double thread across from one corner of the square to the other. Work a row of buttonholing on this double thread.
2 Work each following row into the looped edge of the previous row, reducing the number of stitches to form the design, which is anchored to the fabric on the opposite side.

Filling other squares

1 To strengthen the threads left in squares,

cover them either with weaving or close buttonhole stitch. If you add further decoration with picots, make sure they do not occur at a point where you will be working further bars.
2 To work diagonal lines, take a long stitch from the center to the corner of the square and back again, and fasten off at the back of the center. Cover the diagonal threads by sewing over them or buttonholing to the position of the first bar or arc.
3 To form the bar or arc, take a double thread across for the foundation, cover it with overcast stitch or buttonholing and then complete the diagonal line to the center of the square. The bars or arcs can

be decorated with picots.
4 Alternatively a solid triangular shape can be worked in detached buttonhole stitch from the bar which dissects the diagonal line.
5 On fine fabrics the center of the square can be decorated by working a small back-stitched spider's web over the junction of the threads.

Finishing

Finish off with a simple hemstitch border. For something more elaborate, work several rows of hemstitching and twist the threads into bundles.

Eyelet embroidery

Eyelet embroidery is a form of embroidery which consists of eyelets of different shapes and sizes, with additional surface embroidery and scalloped edging.

During the 18th and 19th centuries when eyelet embroidery was worked in Britain in its original form it was composed of much elaborate, floral surface stitchery, eyelets and larger cut spaces with needle-made lace or drawn thread fillings.

The intricacy of the work gave it a very delicate appearance which was ideal for the beautiful christening robes and bonnets made in that period. Traditionally it was worked in white thread on white fabric such as cambric, cotton or fine linen, lawn or muslin.

Later the method became simpler, using less surface stitchery with more emphasis on eyelets and cut shapes and it became known at that time as "Madeira work", after the island where it became a cottage industry. It was used to decorate dress, lingerie, baby wear and household linen, as it still is today.

The design

Eyelet embroidery need not be confined to white embroidery, but if color is chosen it is best to use matching or toning threads rather than contrasting ones. Traditional eyelet embroidery was always elaborately floral in design. A contemporary design may be made for a simple border by using a geometric arrangement of circles and ovals of various sizes with a little surface stitchery and scalloping. Both floor and wall tiles can give ideas for this type of design.

The fabrics and threads

Although much eyelet embroidery is made by machine nowadays, it is still worth making your own by hand in order to achieve the beautiful delicate results and the wide range of fabrics, threads and designs which can be used.

Choose a firm and fine fabric which will not fray with washing, and match the working thread in quality, texture and color (it can be a different tone). On cotton or linen, use a cotton or fine linen mercerized thread and on silk fabrics, a fine twisted silk.

Stitches and equipment

Only four basic stitches are used in eyelet embroidery – running, overcasting, button-holing and satin stitch.

To make the eyelets you will need a pair of very sharp embroidery scissors and a sharp pointed instrument for piercing the fabric.

Making eyelets

1 To make round eyelets, outline the circle with small running stitches.

2 If the circles are less than $\frac{1}{4}$ inch in diameter, pierce the center and then cover the edge with fine overcasting.

3 For larger circles snip from the center, vertically and horizontally, out to the running stitch. Turn the points of fabric under to the back of the work with the needle and overcast the edge taking the stitches over the folded edge and the running stitch. Cut away the surplus fabric close to the stitching.

4 If several eyelets run close together so that they almost touch, they should be worked in two steps. First work the running stitch along the lower edge of the first hole, cross to the top of the second hole and continue in this way across the design. Complete the circles in the second step. This helps to prevent the piece from

tearing during working and in wear later on.

5 To give a heavier effect, or to make the circles thicker on one side, work several rows of running stitch to pad the area and raise it. Then overcast all around the eyelet, grading the length of the overcasting over the padded area.

6 To make oval and triangular eyelets, work in the same way as for round ones, taking care that the shapes are kept accurate and do not become distorted.

7 When making a slot for ribbon, mark the slot and work around it before cutting the opening. This prevents the hole from pulling out of shape while being worked.

The surface embroidery

This is usually worked. in satin or stem stitch. If you want solid padded shapes to give emphasis or detail to the design, they should be padded by working horizontal satin stitch across the design just inside the outline, with vertical satin stitch to cover the horizontal ones.

Scalloping

This is one of the main features of eyelet embroidery and is used to decorate and finish the work.

1 To make a simple scalloped edge, draw the shapes around a coin or small saucer, ½ inch from the raw edge, or more if the fabric tends to fray.

2 Pad the edge by working several rows of running stitch along the outline, graduating the distance between the stitches in the points of the scallops.

For a more solid or raised effect, use chain stitch for the padding instead of running stitch.

3 Cover the padding with closely worked buttonholing, working from left to right and with the looped edge of the stitch to the outside. Keep the stitches as even in tension as possible and do not pull the working thread too tight or the work will pucker. Make the stitches quite small in

the points of the scallops, increasing in size around the curves to emphasize their symmetry.

4 To finish off a length of thread, take a few running stitches through the padding on the unworked section and fasten off. Join on the new length in a similar way, bringing the needle up through the loop of the last buttonhole stitch.

5 When all the buttonholing is worked, cut away the surplus fabric close to the stitches using very sharp scissors.

6 To make a more elaborate scalloped edge, draw a pattern of the design, including about three repeats and then cut it out of cardboard. You can then use this as a template to draw the shapes along the entire edge.

HEDEBO

Hedebo is a form of white embroidery of Danish origin. It dates from the 16th century when the peasant women of Heden, a flat part of Denmark, used to decorate their homespun linens with it.

Types of Hedebo

There are three basic types of Hedebo.

The oldest and most traditional was adapted from wood carvings and usually consisted of formal floral shapes combining surface embroidery with a few open and drawn thread fillings. Most of the surface embroidery was in chain stitch and the finished effect was soft and graceful.

The second type of Hedebo evolved around 1840 when the original floral shapes and cut work were somewhat restrained and the embroidery lost some of its original character. Further cut and drawn thread work was added, usually in squares, making the whole design more formal and geometric.

The third type of Hedebo dates from about 1850 when it became quite popular and gradually lost its peasant-like quality. In modern Hedebo, designs became more conventional and the spaces were cut instead of drawn and cut, and filled in with more elaborate lace stitchery.

Designs for old Hedebo

Old Hedebo is traditionally worked on a close handwoven linen in a medium weight linen thread.

The main open shapes are formed by cutting and leaving two threads alternately, both vertically and horizontally, from the back of the work. The edge of the shape is then made firm by overcasting which is worked in groups of two over the horizontal and vertical bars. The spaces are enriched with more decorative stitches and the shapes are outlined with a double row of small close chain stitches.

The working method for the second form of Hedebo is very similar, with the open drawn squares being arranged in diagonal lines to form a diamond pattern, often interspersed with floral-type surface embroidery.

Designs for modern Hedebo

Designs for modern Hedebo usually consist of an arrangement or pattern of circular, oval or lozenge-shaped cut spaces which are strengthened and then outlined with buttonhole stitch.

Choose a fine, firm linen for the work with a matching linen thread. If a linen thread is unobtainable, use a fine coton à broder or pearl cotton.

The shapes are filled with a variety of lace stitches which are looped, twisted or buttonholed into the foundation row of buttonholing. Buttonholed pyramids are a feature of this type of work and these can be incorporated into the larger shapes or used as edgings to decorate the work. Satin stitch and eyelets, rather like eyelet embroidery, can be added and the work can be finished with a needlepoint lace edging. This form of Hedebo is often used for the decoration of collars and cuffs.

1 Transfer the design onto the fabric either by basting around an arrangement of cut paper shapes or by using a very finely pointed pencil and outlining the shapes with minute dots.

2 Work a double row of running stitches

around the outlines.
3 Cut away the fabric within the design, leaving a margin of about $\frac{1}{4}$ inch to $\frac{1}{8}$ inch for smaller spaces.

Clip into this margin and turn it to the wrong side. Outline the space with Hedebo buttonhole stitch (see below), making sure that the fabric is turned under the needle and that the stitch is worked through both layers. Trim away surplus fabric close to the stitches.

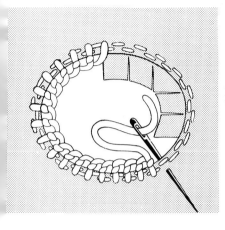

4 Fill the spaces and then add the surface embroidery.
5 Finish the work with a narrow hemstitched edge or with needlepoint lace, constructed of Hedebo buttonholing to form loops, pyramids or small rings.

Hedebo buttonholing
The buttonholing used for outlining the shapes is slightly different from regular buttonholing in that it is worked in two separate steps.
1 Hold the fabric so that the edge to be worked is away from you and insert the needle into the fabric from underneath. Draw the thread through until a small loop remains.
2 Slip the needle through the loop and pull both stitch and loop tight.

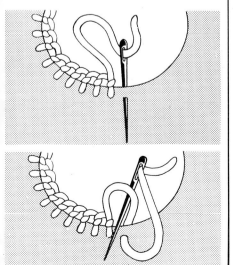

3 To join in a new thread, slip it under the last loop of thread worked and place it alongside the first thread. Work six or seven stitches over both threads and then cut off the remainder of the first thread.

Filling stitches
Circles
1 Work an inner circle of Hedebo buttonholing loosely inside the first circle, placing one stitch into every third stitch of the first circle. To obtain a loose effect, omit the final sharp pull to each stitch.
2 When the inner circle is completed, overcast or whip the looped edges.

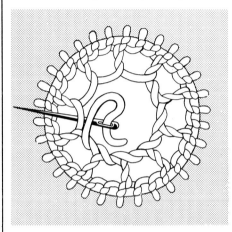

3 Fill the center of the circle by working a woven or backstitched wheel over the four or six threads anchored into the last row of buttonholing.

Circles and lozenge shapes
Fill circles and lozenge shapes by constructing a number of bars with two or three threads across the shape. Cover these with close Hedebo buttonhole stitch.

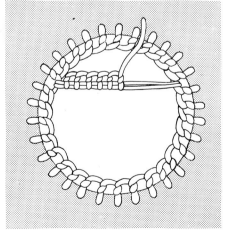

Pyramids
These are a characteristic feature of modern Hedebo and are constructed of Hedebo buttonholing stitches in increasing or decreasing rows. They can be worked singly to fill a small space or in groups of four to fill an oval or pear-shaped space.
1 Prepare the edge with a foundation row of buttonholing.
2 Start the pyramid by working from left to right, working one stitch less at the ends of each row.
3 Continue in this way until the top of the pyramid is reached, then slip the needle down the right side to start the next pyramid.

Six-pointed star
This is worked as a separate motif to be used as an insertion.
1 Wrap the thread around a pencil several times and secure the circle with a stitch.
2 Remove the circle from the pencil and buttonhole over it. This forms the foundation circle.
3 Work another round of buttonholing, counting the stitches carefully to make a multiple of six.
4 Work a pyramid onto each multiple number of buttonhole stitches, making six points in all.
5 Secure the shape in position with a single stitch at each point.

FAGGOTING

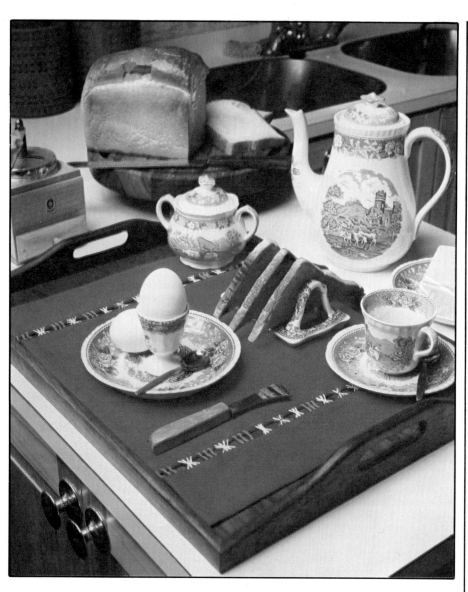

Placemats
Size
$15\frac{3}{4}$ in $\times$ $12\frac{1}{2}$ in.

Fabric required
For four mats:
$\frac{3}{4}$ yd firm cotton or linen, 36 in wide (or you can use remnants and cut the panels in sizes to suit the fabric available).

You will also need
Stranded embroidery thread to match the fabric.
Matching sewing thread.
Crewel embroidery needle.
Four strips of firm paper, $12\frac{1}{2}$ in $\times$ $1\frac{1}{2}$ in.

Preparing the fabric
1 Cut the fabric across the width to make two pieces $13\frac{1}{2}$ inches $\times$ 36 inches. Cut these pieces in half lengthwise to make four pieces each $13\frac{1}{2}$ inches $\times$ 18 inches.
2 Cut each of the four pieces into three, with two sections $13\frac{1}{2}$ inches wide and one section 11 inches wide.
3 Turn under $\frac{1}{2}$ inch on the wrong side around the edge of all the pieces and make narrow hems with mitered corners. Hem by hand the two opposite sides of the large sections and one long side and two short sides of the smaller sections. Leave the remaining edges basted in position.
4 For each mat, place the basted hem of one small section on the edge of a strip of firm paper so that it overlaps slightly. Baste in place. Overlap the basted hem of the larger section onto the opposite edge of the paper and baste leaving a gap $\frac{1}{2}$ inch wide. Repeat this procedure on the opposite edge of the larger section and on the second smaller section.

Working the faggoting
1 Mount the fabric into a hoop.
2 Work the faggoting between the basted edges, following one of the stitch patterns shown in the illustration. Make sure that the stitches worked into the edges of the fabric catch the hems securely.
3 When all the faggoting is completed, press the finished mats.

Faggoting is an attractive method of joining two pieces of fabric together using an open-work design. It is particularly useful for table linens for which you do not necessarily need the strength of a regular seam and where a seam line would spoil the effect. For example, if you are making a tablecloth from 36 inch wide dress fabric or 48 inch wide home furnishing fabric and you need to join panels to make it the right width for your table, you could join the panels with faggoting. The panels need not be confined to long strips but could be cut to make an attractive added feature. Faggoting can be used on both square and rounded shapes providing the edges to be joined lie along the grain of the fabric. If you work them on the bias, they will not lie flat.

Many of the stitches used in faggoting are common embroidery stitches and they are simple to work. Their success depends however on keeping their size and keeping the spaces between the edges absolutely even. For this reason it is worth mounting the work onto a frame.

Faggoting can be worked in most kinds of embroidery thread of whatever weight will suit the fabric you are working on. You might also use a fine crochet yarn. The instructions given below are for making the mat shown in the photograph, although they can easily be adapted for a tablecloth.

STITCH PATTERNS FOR FAGGOTING

NEEDLEMADE LACE

Lace making using a needle is quite different from lace made with an implement, such as a crochet hook or tatting shuttle, and it should not be confused with bobbin lace (sometimes called pillow lace), because it is made on a pillow. Needlemade lace is an old craft which was popular in all European countries in the mid-15th and 16th centuries. It is directly derived from the elaborate cut and drawn work of the 15th century which was often used for ecclesiastical purposes and to decorate the household articles and fashionable garments of the nobility.

The stitches

The Italian name for needlemade lace is "Punto in aria," meaning stitches in the air, and the lace itself is made with nothing more than a foundation, a needle and thread. The stitches used are merely variations of simple embroidery stitches and those most used are buttonhole (or blanket) stitch in one of its various forms, and a number of knotted stitches.

The threads

The thread should be suitable in weight for the fabric on which the edging is to be placed. If you are working on linen, use a linen thread, single-strand embroidery thread or pearlized cotton crochet yarn. If the fabric is heavy, such as tweed, a heavier cord or cotton yarn would be suitable. For working the edgings use a tapestry needle of a suitable size.

First method

This method could be used for narrow borders to decorate table linen, lampshades or perhaps a dress. It is worked directly onto the folded edge of the fabric.
1 Join your thread into the side of the edge to be decorated and take a tiny stitch into the fold about $\frac{3}{8}$ inch further along point A, leaving a small loop.
2 Return to the starting point and make another stitch. Go to point A again, make another stitch, keeping the loops the same size. Return to the starting point again. You now have four equal loops, forming a small scallop.

3 Work over the scallop in close buttonhole stitch.
4 Make a second loop in exactly the same way and then lay the threads for a third scallop but work only halfway across them in buttonhole stitch.
5 Make a loop from the center of the third scallop to the center of the second one, and then from the center of the second one to the center of the first one. Repeat this until there are three loops in each of these two scallops thus forming a second row.

6 Work over the first loop and halfway over the second loop in the second row.
7 Make a loop from the middle of the second scallop in the second row into the middle of the first one. Repeat until there are three loops in the scallop and then work over them in buttonhole stitch and over the half loops left in the first and second rows, using a buttonhole stitch.

Second method

This border can be worked into a hem or onto a foundation of buttonholing. Work all rows from left to right and fasten off the thread at the end of each row.
1 Start by working a row of spaced double-knotted buttonhole stitches into the edge of the fabric.
2 For the second row, work the same stitch, putting each one into a loop between the knots of the first row.
3 For the third row, work two double knotted stitches into the first loop, an ordinary single buttonhole stitch into the next loop, and continue alternating in this way to the end of the row.
4 For the last row, work two ordinary buttonhole stitches into the loop on each side of the single stitch on the third row and, with two double knotted stitches, into each space between the double knots.

Working a separate strip

If you prefer to make the lace in a separate strip and then sew it on later, a way which is more convenient for a large or heavy item, use a piece of stiff linen or bookbinding cloth as a foundation. The strip should be the same length as the piece of lace required and about 2 inches wider.
1 Draw a line along the strip about $\frac{1}{2}$ inch from the top edge, using a ruler.
2 Couch a double thread of crochet yarn or other firm thread along the line, using a contrasting color for the stitches which hold the thread. This will make it easier to remove.
3 Work the lace onto the couched thread and remove the small stitches holding the thread when the lace is completed.

VENETIAN LACE

Make a border with stars or buttonholed pyramids to form a circle.

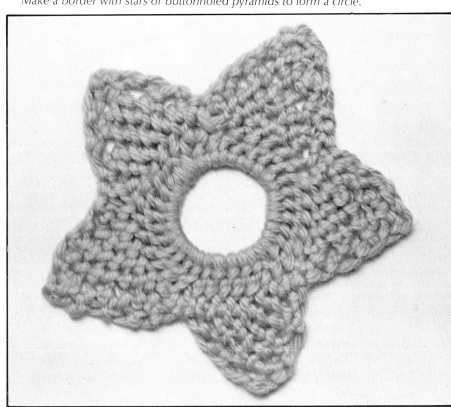

Venetian lace is the oldest type of lace made with a needle. The motifs are geometric in design and, like the narrow edgings described in the previous chapter, they are made with fine, closely worked buttonhole stitches and knotted stitches. They are worked onto couched threads which are held with temporary stitches on a firm foundation while the lace is being made.

The finished motifs, depending on the weight of the thread used, could be sewn onto lingerie, blouses and dresses, and onto sheets, pillowcases and table linen.

The threads and equipment

Linen thread is usually the best for working most types of lace, although fine crochet cotton, pearl cotton, and coton à broder are suitable.

For the couching, use a linen thread or mercerized crochet cotton, and for the final padding, a soft thread such as Sylko Size 5.

You will also need fine tapestry and crewel needles to suit the weight of the thread and a pair of finely pointed embroidery scissors.

For marking the design and for the foundation you will need either white paint and strong black paper with a matte texture, or India ink or a black felt-tipped pen and tracing paper. Both kinds of foundation should be backed with strong muslin or book-binding cloth. Alternatively you can use book binding cloth alone as the foundation.

Marking the design

1 Start by planning a well-balanced geometric design on graph paper, and consider how the lines are to be joined and the spaces filled. One way of doing this is to draw parts of the design in close double lines which separate and.then rejoin them. The spaces can be filled with bars or bridges.

2 Draw the design accurately onto the foundation.

Tracing the design

1 Trace over the design by outlining it with couched threads. Keep the threads as continuous as possible and, where they are used double, insure that they lie evenly side by side.

Where one line branches to another, divide the thread and couch it as far as necessary and then double back to the starting point. Where one line touches another, thread the couching under and back again so that the pattern is joined.

2 Secure the couching to the foundation with small temporary stitches, preferably worked in a contrasting color to make them easier to remove. However, if the lace is being worked in white it is better to use white thread, as the color may leave traces.

Filling in the design

1 Fill in the various spaces of the design by using one of the buttonhole stitches given below. Be as inventive as you like, for it is the variety of the stitches which give reticella lace its character.
2 When the filling is complete, make the final bars or bridges to link those lines which do not touch each other. These can be worked by buttonholing or by oversewing.
3 Start by laying several threads evenly across the space to be filled by taking small stitches in the outline threads on each side. Cover these threads with buttonholing or oversewing.

4 If you want a wider bar, work buttonhole stitches along both edges and decorate the bar with rings, picots or other bars.

Outlining the design
This is the step which gives the final touch to the lace. The whole design is now outlined in close buttonholing, using a fine thread to bring it to life.
To give dimension and emphasis to the various parts, work over a couple of strands of soft padding thread. Where one part appears to pass over another, work the part underneath first.
When joining in and fastening off threads, take a few neat overcast stitches into the part of the outlining nearest to you. These stitches will be worked in with the final outlining, which should cover them completely and also help strengthen the finished lace.

Finishing
The last and most exciting stage is the removal of the lace from the foundation, which is done quite simply by cutting and removing the stitches which hold down the couched thread.

The stitches
Here are just a few of the basic stitches which can be used to create needlemade lace. You can invent numerous patterns with the interplay of the various stitches and the spaces created by them and embellish them further with picots and loops to give greater dexterity to the work. Basic buttonhole stitch, single and double knot stitch and bullion stitch are all described later in the dictionary of stitches.

Knotted buttonhole stitch
1 Work a row of buttonhole stitches from left to right over the couched thread.
2 Work a second row, from right to left, reversing the stitch into the loop made by

the first stitch. Work each stitch at a slight angle, pulling tight each knot thus formed before continuing to the next stitch. Two or three buttonhole stitches can often be drawn together by working this stitch over a whole group at once.

Corded buttonhole stitch
1 Work a row of spaced buttonhole stitches from right to left.

2 Work a row of overcast stitches from left to right over the loops of the previous row.
3 Repeat these rows alternately for the desired length. When working the third row, be sure that you stitch into the loop of the buttonholing, not into the overcasting.

Twisted stitches
These give a light and airy appearance to the work. It is important to keep the tension as even as possible and the stitches themselves carefully spaced. One method of working this is to overcast the loops, as for corded buttonhole stitch. Alternatively, they can be built up into a pyramid

formation, each row having one less twisted stitch than the previous one.

Picots
1 To work a picot, make a second buttonhole stitch into the loop of the last stitch worked and then insert the needle into the loop of this second stitch just made.
2 Twist the working thread around the needle, draw up the knot and pass the needle through the loop of the original buttonhole stitch, ready to continue the row of buttonholing. The knots should twist and form into a small circle.

SHADOW WORK

Shadow work is a type of embroidery which relies for effect on a filling stitch, worked on the wrong side of a transparent fabric so that the color of the working thread shows through in a subdued tint to the right side of the work.

It is usually worked on a very fine fabric such as organdy, organza, fine linen lawn, cotton lawn, muslin and crepe de chine in a soft shade.

Until this century it was always worked in white on a white fabric with double back-stitch (a variation of herringbone). The threads of the stitches cross on the back of the work to give an opaque quality on the right side.

In more modern work the introduction of color has changed the effect to produce an opalescent look and this type of work lends itself well to such articles as baby clothes, lingerie, party dresses and aprons as well as on more delicate table linen, lampshades and curtains.

The design

Designs for shadow work should consist of narrow shapes which have simple outlines. Traditionally the work was always floral in design with the addition of a little surface stitchery but nowadays abstract shapes of suitable proportions can be used.

The shapes are nevertheless restricted in width by the double backstitch or herringbone stitch which fills and outlines them. To transfer the design onto the fabric, simply place the fabric over the design with the right side facing down and trace over the lines of the design with a fine pencil.

Threads and needles

Choose a fine thread – either pure silk, 6-strand floss or fine coton à broder – in a color darker or brighter than the fabric so that you can achieve the desired finished effect.

Use fine crewel or between needles.

The working method

When the design has been traced onto the wrong side of the fabric, work all the main areas in close herringbone stitch (or double backstitch). Extra wide shapes can be filled in with two rows of herringbone, but this is best avoided.

Close herringbone stitch is worked in the same way as ordinary herringbone but with the stitches touching each other at the top and bottom, thus building up two parallel lines of backstitch on the front of the work with the opaque area between them.

Form the stitches as evenly as possible, following the outline of the shapes and working into all the corners and points in order to complete the outline accurately on the right side.

Work the stitches slightly smaller and closer together on the inside of curves and slightly larger on the outside. Take care that the stitches do not slope and always remain perpendicular to the base line.

When all the main areas are filled in, any additional stitchery such as linear detail, eyelets and spider's web wheels can be worked on the right side.

Because the fabric is transparent, take care to conceal all ends of threads.

Do not use knots to finish but darn all ends back into the work securely and neatly.

French shadow work

This is extremely easy to work and produces quick and attractive results.

The motif most normally used is the square, which is marked onto the fabric by drawing a thread from side to side to insure an accurate outline.

The squares are first worked one way and then the other, taking up an equal number of threads each time. The threads must be counted carefully so that the blocks of stitches are perfectly even.

Several variations of the square can be developed and the Greek key design is always a good stand-by.

Indian shadow work

This has almost the same effect as traditional shadow work but a slightly different working method is used.

Instead of the stitches crossing on the back of the work they are taken from side to side, picking up a small amount of fabric each time and zig-zagging between the lines of the design.

Take care to pick up a small stitch each time so that the threads will not be too openly spaced on the back of the work, thus spoiling the shadow effect on the front.

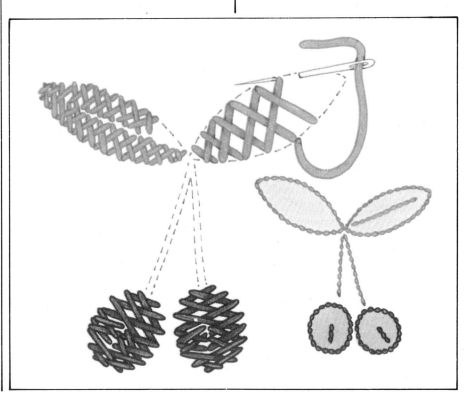

Shadow work for sheers

Light as air and delicate as spring flowers, this curtain with its shadow work motifs has a romantic prettiness far more attractive than any net curtain that can be bought. Only three simple stitches are used: backstitch, satin stitch and double back or closed herringbone stitch.

Fabric required

Length of fine pale green nylon or organdy to fit window, plus $1\frac{1}{2}$ in turnings at top and bottom and $\frac{1}{4}$ in turnings at side.

You will also need

D.M.C. 6-Strand Floss in the following colors and quantities (to work 8 motifs): 2 skeins each 320 laurel green and white; 1 skein 776 blossom pink.
Alternatively, D.M.C. Pearl Cotton No. 8: one 10 grm ball each 894 carnation, 989 grass green and white.

Embroidery hoop.
Tracing paper.
Crewel needle No. 7.

Transferring the motifs

Two complete motifs are illustrated to size in the tracing pattern. Trace the motifs and transfer them to the fabric either with dressmakers' carbon paper or by outlining with small basting stitches.
Alternate the motifs evenly along the edge of the fabric, placing them above the final hem turning.

The design

1 No special skill is required for shadow work but it is important to work neatly so that the double lines of backstitch lie closely together. This will be easier to do if the work is held in an embroidery hoop.
2 Using 3 strands of floss throughout,

follow the working chart as a guide.
3 Double backstitch, or closed herringbone stitch, can be worked either from the right or the wrong side of the fabric. Figure 1 shows how a small backstitch is worked alternately on each side of the traced double lines. The dotted lines on the diagram show the formation of the thread on the wrong side of the fabric, with the color showing delicately through.
4 Figure 2 shows closed herringbone stitch worked on the wrong side of the fabric with no spaces left between the stitches. Both methods achieve the same result. Whichever method you choose, take care that the work is as neat on the back as on the front.
5 To finish off, press the embroidery on the wrong side, turn up the side and bottom hems and make a heading and a casing for the curtain rod at the top.

Color and stitch guide.

Figure 1 Method of working double backstitch on the right side of the fabric.

Figure 2 Method of working closed herringbone stitch on the wrong side of the fabric.

Backstitch.

Satin stitch.

Tracing pattern for motif A.

Tracing pattern for motif B.

Organdy apron

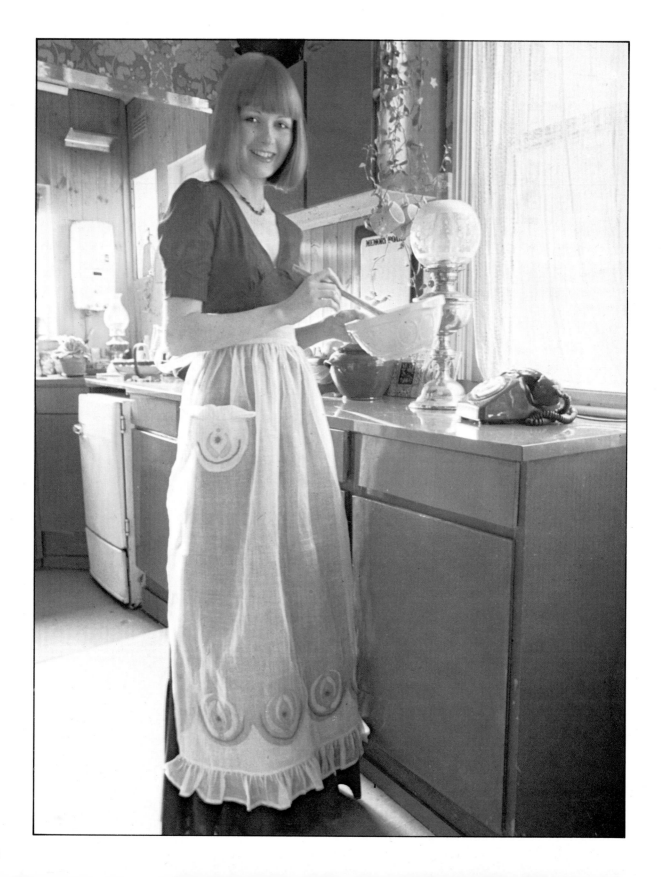

Size

The length can be adjusted to fit all sizes.

Fabric required

1¼ yards cotton organdy, 44 inches wide.

You will also need

Matching pure silk thread.
6-strand embroidery floss in a darker and lighter shade of main color.
Pearl cotton embroidery thread in a lighter shade of main color.
Fine crewel needle.
Fine tapestry needle.

Cutting out

Fold the fabric in half lengthwise placing the selvages together. Cut out the pieces as shown in the chart.

Making the apron

1 Place the facing strip along the bottom edge of the main section and baste together all around the edge. This now forms the wrong side of the apron.
2 Using a sharp pencil and a small plate or saucer as a guide, draw a scalloped edge on the wrong side of the fabric along the top edge of the facing. Start from the center-front and work outward to the sides insuring that the scallops are evenly balanced.

	right side		wrong side

3 With the tapestry needle and pure silk thread, work pin stitching along the scalloped line on the wrong side of the fabric. Use sharp embroidery scissors to trim the excess fabric back to the stitching line.
4 Place the fabric, wrong side facing up, over the motif and trace it, placing one motif above each scallop as shown.

5 Still working on the wrong side, fill in the two inner shapes in herringbone stitch, using the darker shade of stranded floss and the fine crewel needle. Keep the top and bottom of the stitch equal in width so that the work will be even on the right side.
6 Work the two outershapes in the same way, using the lighter shade of the stranded floss.
7 Using the fine pearl cotton complete the surface stitchery on the right side of the work.

Work a backstitch spider's web in the middle.
8 For the stitching enclosing the bottom of the motif, work a graduating line of fine satin stitch, ⅛ inch apart, starting with a very small stitch and gradually getting wider then tapering off to a very small stitch at the beginning of the row.
9 On the satin stitch row work a row of raised chain band, making it a double row where the line thickens in the center and tapering it by starting and finishing with several stem or split stitches.
Work a motif onto the pocket in the same way.

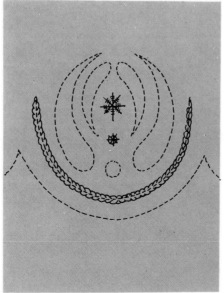

The ruffle

10 Finish each side of the apron with a ½ inch hem.

Join the pieces for the ruffle along the narrow edge with a French seam.
Make a narrow hem along the short ends and bottom edge of the ruffle. Work a row of gathering along the top edge.

11 Remove the basting thread from the bottom edge of the apron. With right sides together baste the top edge of the ruffle to the bottom of the apron, arranging the gathers evenly and leaving the edge of of the facing free. Machine stitch, taking ½ inch turnings.
12 Press the turnings upward, turn under the edge of the facing and place the fold to the stitch line. Hem into place.

The pocket

13 Prepare the pocket ruffle in the same way as for the main ruffle.

Place the ruffle, wrong side down, on the right side of the pocket so that the raw edges are even along the top. Arrange the gathers evenly and baste in position.

14 Work a very narrow hem along one long edge of the pocket facing. Place the facing on to the top of the pocket so that the raw edges are even along the top and sides. Baste and machine stitch along the top and sides, taking $\frac{1}{2}$ inch turnings. Turn the facing onto the wrong side of the pocket and press.

15 Turn under the remaining sides of the pocket. Place the pocket in position onto the apron. Baste and machine stitch.

The waistband

16 Fold under the short ends of the waistband for $\frac{1}{2}$ inch onto the wrong side and baste. Fold the waistband in half lengthwise.

17 Try on the apron for length and adjust it at the top edge if necessary. Work a row of gathering along the top edge. With right sides together, pin the gathered edge to one long side of the waistband, arranging the gathers evenly. Baste in place.

18 Make narrow hems along the two long sides and one short side of the apron ties. Place the fourth side to the ends of the waistband, gathering the fullness as shown below.

19 Stitch, taking $\frac{1}{2}$ inch turnings from the left edge at the top of the tie, across the front and over the tie at the right edge.

Fold under the remaining edges of the waistband and hem neatly but firmly to the stitch line.

Cutting layout for apron

| | | | 45¼ in | | |

FOLD

Waist-band

6 in

Bottom facing

4 in

15 in

Main section

35 in

22 in

Pocket

Pocket facing

Bottom ruffle
Use 6 in of one layer for pocket ruffle

3½ in

Waistband ties

3½ in

SELVAGES

Tracing pattern for embroidery

Stitching a sampler

For centuries the sampler was an essential part of every girl's education. Many survive today as beautiful examples of fine needlework. Now you can work your own sampler in the traditional manner. Nearly 20 different stitches, including drawn thread work, are included to make this sampler a technical exercise for the experienced needleworker as well as for the beginner. Add your name and date of completion at top or bottom for a really authentic touch.

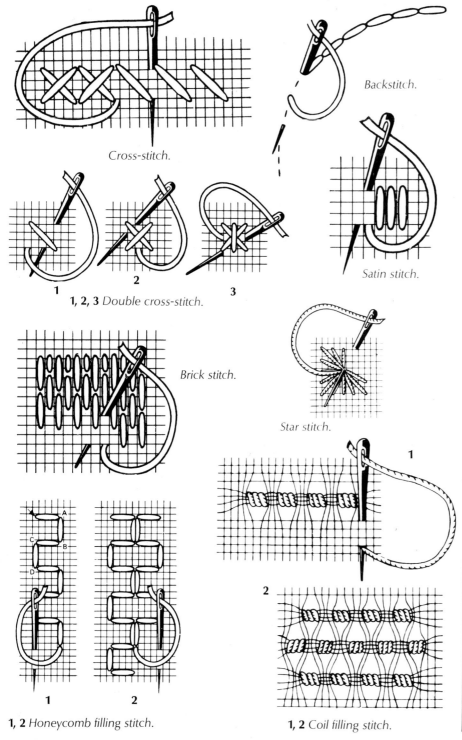

Cross-stitch.

Backstitch.

1, 2, 3 *Double cross-stitch.*

Satin stitch.

Brick stitch.

Star stitch.

1, 2 *Honeycomb filling stitch.*

1, 2 *Coil filling stitch.*

Fabric required
36 in beige medium weight evenweave fabric, 21 threads to 1 in, 59 in wide.

You will also need
D.M.C. 6-strand floss in the following colors and quantities: 3 skeins tapestry shade 610, 2 skeins each tapestry shades 3013, 3012, 3046; 1 skein each tapestry shades 932, 931, 930, ecru, 3045, geranium 948, 352 and 249.
Picture frame with mounting board or cardboard to fit embroidery.
Tapestry needles Nos. 20 and 24 for 6 and 3 strands respectively.

The design
1 Cut a piece from the fabric to measure 36 inches square. Mark the centers both ways with a line of basting stitches.
2 Diagram 1 gives slightly more than half the design with the center indicated by black arrows.
Note It is important to remember when working the design that each background square on the diagram represents 2 threads of the evenweave fabric.
3 Use 6 strands of thread and needle size 20 for Swedish darning, satin stitch, couching and oblique loop stitch. Use 3 strands and needle size 24 for the rest of the embroidery.
4 Diagram 2 shows the Swedish darning and satin stitch tree. The background lines on this diagram indicate the threads of the fabric.
5 Begin working the sampler centrally with four-sided stitch filling, 2 threads down and 6 threads to the right of the crossed basting stitches. Follow Diagram 1 and the stitch and color key for the main part of the design.
Repeat, reversing the design, from the lower black arrow to complete the second half of the sampler.
6 Couching is worked horizontally between satin stitch C9 on the diagram.
7 Once the embroidery for Diagram 1 has been completed, work Diagram 2 in the position indicated, following the key for the design and stitches used. The four drawn thread borders are worked one on each side of the completed design, linked by woven bars and oblique loop stitch as shown in the photograph.

Finishing the sampler
Press the completed sampler on the wrong side. Place it centrally over the mounting board, fold the surplus fabric to the back of the board and secure it all around with pins stuck into the edge of the board. Lace the fabric across the back both ways with strong thread. Remove the pins and mount the sampler in a frame.

KEY

O	948	
X	352	
▲	249	
/	3013	
V	932	Cross-stitch
=	931	
✦	930	
⊙	3046	
◑	3045	
●	610	

‡	931	
❙	930	
❙	3045	Back-stitch
†	610	
✚	3013	

	A	
1	948	Double
2	3013	cross-stitch
3	3012	
4	3045	

	B	
5	3013	Star stitch
6	3046	
7	3045	

	C	
8	ecru	Satin stitch
9	3045	

	D	
10	931	Brick stitch
11	ecru	

12	249	Honeycomb filling stitch
13	3012	Coil filling stitch
14	930	Four sided stitch filling
15	—	Swedish darning and satin stitch tree

DIAGRAM 1 ▶

KEY
1	3012	} Swedish
2	3013	darning
3	3046	
4	3012	Satin stitch

1, 2, 3, 4 Four sided stitch.

Oblique loop stitch woven bars.

Zigzag hem stitch
and four sided stitch.

Interlaced hemstitch border.

Hemstitch and
satin stitch border.

Hemstitch and four sided stitch border.

Couching.

The completed sampler is laced across
the mounting board with strong thread.

DIAGRAM 2 ▶

NEEDLEPOINT
Basic equipment

Needlepoint is a relaxing form of embroidery. It requires little mental effort and can be most effective when worked in one stitch. Carried out on a stiff, open-weave fabric, it is hard-wearing for use in the home as chair seat covers, stool tops, pillows, lamp bases, etc. It can also be made into exciting and useful accessories, such as belts, bags and slippers. Its use for clothes, however, is more restricted because of its stiffness although it could be made up into a simple garment such as a vest. Needlepoint is more properly known as canvas work or – mistakenly – tapestry work. Tapestry is the name given to a form of weaving, usually of a pictorial kind and this has led to the canvases sold with the design already painted on also being called tapestries.

The equipment

Needlepoint can be done without a frame if you are able to maintain an even tension throughout, although it frequently does become distorted since the heat of the hands affects the stiffening in the threads of the canvas. This usually results in the work having to be pinned and stretched over layers of damp blotting paper once completed in order to restore it to its former shape.

It is much better to use an embroidery frame or a canvas work frame to prevent this and also to protect the canvas from being creased or crumpled while being worked on as this affects the rigidity that keeps the stitches in place.

Types of canvas frame

There are two types of canvas frame, the flat bar and the screw bar. The flat bar frame is more suitable for large pieces of work using conventional stitches and threads because the canvas is rolled up as the work progresses. It is not so suitable for more adventurous designs using wooden beads, rings, plastic or leather shapes, because these additions prevent the work from rolling smoothly.

The screw bar frame has adjustable side pieces which fit into rollers at both ends. This kind of frame has to be large enough to take the fully extended canvas since it cannot be rolled.

An old picture frame or artist's painting stretcher can sometimes be used success-

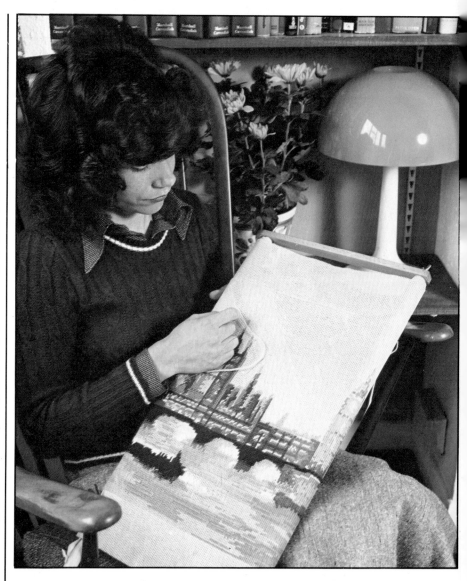

fully as a substitute frame. To attach the canvas to it, machine-stitch wide tape over the edge of the canvas to strengthen it and then fix firmly to the frame with thumb tacks or staples placed at $\frac{1}{2}$ inch intervals.

An embroidery hoop is suitable only for small pieces of work where the part of canvas enclosed by the rings will be cut off since it may have become distorted from the pressure.

The canvas

Canvas is made from linen, hemp, cotton or gauze. Single (or mono) canvas has the threads interwoven singly and is the type most often used because any type of stitch can be worked without difficulty.

Double canvas has the threads woven in pairs and is normally used when fine detail and small stitching are being used in the design. The stitches are mostly worked over the pair of threads for the background of the design and over one thread of the pair for the detailed sections.

The number of the mesh indicates the number of threads to the inch.

Good quality wide-meshed linen scrim can be used instead of canvas where you want a more pliable effect and this can be worked with all the usual stitches but often with much more exciting results.

Fine wire mesh and wire gauze have also been used for experimental canvas work.

The needles

Tapestry needles, which are blunt-ended with a large eye to enable the thread to be pulled through easily, are sold in a variety of sizes to suit the canvas and thread used. Before threading a needle with yarn, hold the yarn up to the light to see the direction of the fibers (drawing the thread through your fingers will show you if the fibers are lying in the right direction). Thread the yarn into the needle so that the fibers are lying away from the threaded end. In this way, the fibers will be stroked downward when they are pulled through the canvas, thus reducing the tension on the yarn and insuring a smoother finish to the work. You will also need two pairs of good scissors, one for cutting the canvas and paper for designs, and another small sharp-pointed pair for cutting thread. A pair of tweezers will be very useful if you have to unpick any stitches.

The designs

In Victorian times needlepoint was used for elaborate pictorial designs, such as wreaths of full-blown roses, baskets of fruit and other still life scenes, usually worked in tent stitch or cross stitch. Today, however, needlepoint is most attractive when it is used for geometric designs which allow a variety of textures, threads and stitches to be used.

Cut paper shapes arranged in a geometric pattern are perhaps the easiest form of designing for a beginner.

Squared paper or graph paper is best for drawing the final designs for needlepoint, because each square of paper can be used to denote one stitch worked over two threads of the canvas. It is possible to buy graph paper with squares corresponding to those of the canvas. This allows you to work out intricate designs in detail and in advance.

A useful economy is to copy the design onto waxed paper or tracing paper, and to place this over the graph paper to redraw and "square off". In this way the graph paper can be re-used several times.

To transfer the design onto the canvas, tack the tracing to the canvas around the edges and then baste along each line of the design using a colored basting thread and small stitches.

An alternate method is to outline the tracing with black poster paint, India ink or felt-tipped pen. Then center the canvas over the design and trace the outline onto the canvas. It is advisable to mark the center of each edge of both the tracing and the canvas so that they can be matched accurately, and also to secure the tracing with thumb tacks if you are using this method.

The threads

It is extremely important that the yarns and threads used for needlepoint should be right for the mesh of the canvas so that the stitches cover it completely. A large mesh canvas is obviously unsuitable for fine yarn and vice versa.

The type of thread depends largely on the nature of the work and how it will be used. Wool is the traditional thread for needle-point and it is the most durable. Crewel wool is sold especially for needlepoint and it can be used with two or three strands to suit the mesh. Knitting yarn can also be used if crewel yarn is not available. There is an almost unlimited choice of other threads, too – pearl cotton in various weights, stranded thread, twisted silks, tapestry yarn, single-strand embroidery thread, soft thread, lurex and even string.

Needlepoint stitches

Key to Chart
1 Padded satin stitch
2 Hungarian stitch
3 Large cross stitch worked alternately with Hungarian
4 Long-legged cross stitch
5 Brick stitch
6 Long-legged cross stitch
7 Norwich stitch
8 Large cross stitch and straight cross stitch
9 Paris stitch
10 Eye stitch
Background: tent stitch

There are a great number of needlepoint stitches, many of which are similar to those used in regular embroidery. Here are a few of the most useful.

Smyrna or double cross
This is double cross stitch worked in two directions. Work cross stitch over four threads and then complete each stitch by working another cross stitch vertically

over the first stitch as shown.

Long-legged cross
This is a useful stitch because it .can be worked in horizontal rows from left to right and from right to left, or in vertical rows from the top down and from the bottom up. Work as shown in the diagram, always beginning and ending each row with a regular cross stitch. If used to fill in a background, the rows can be worked alternately in each direction. The long-

legged cross stitch can also be combined with the tent stitch worked in alternate rows.

Continental stitch

This looks very much like a half cross-stitch but is worked to give more cover on the back of the canvas. It can be worked from right to left, in vertical rows or diagonal rows. It is a good background stitch and throws more chunky stitches into relief.

Knot stitch

This is another variation of cross stitch with one of the obliques worked over three threads and the other oblique worked over one thread to tie it. A useful filling stitch, it produces a good texture for backgrounds.

Rice stitch

This is a development of cross stitch. Work the crosses in thick yarn over four threads. Then, using a finer thread in a contrasting color or texture, work a single diagonal over each corner. Work these stitches in two horizontal rows, tying down the two upper corners of each cross in the first row and the two lower corners in rhe second row.

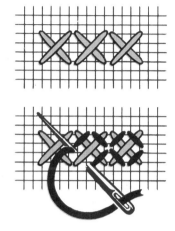

Hungarian stitch

This is a simple stitch which is more effective when worked in two colors or two textures. It consists of straight stitches worked in groups of three. For the first row, work the first stitch over two threads, the second over four threads and the third over two threads. Leave two threads and repeat to the end of the row. Work the second row as for the first, fitting the longer stitches into the spaces left by the previous row as shown.

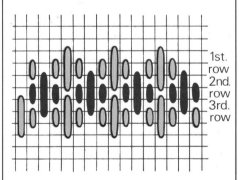

Paris stitch

This is a good background filling stitch made by working alternately over one and then over three threads of the canvas in alternate rows from left to right and right

to left. The short stitches in the second row fit in under the long stitches of the rows on each side.

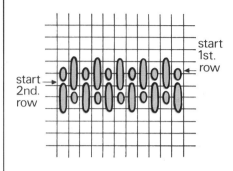

Eye stitch

This consists of 16 stitches worked over eight threads, all radiating from the same center hole.

Norwich stitch

This is not as complicated as it appears. It can be worked over any size square, providing that the square consists of an uneven number of threads. Start at point 1 and take a straight stitch to point 2. Go to the opposite corner and take a stitch from point 3 to point 4. Continue in this way around the square, taking stitches between the points shown on the diagram, giving the effect of a square on the diagonal.

Needlepoint sampler

This pillow can be worked as a sampler to practice many different stitches comprising an interesting collection of textures. The simple use of one color also emphasizes the variation of stitches, although other colors may be used.

Size
17 inches.

Fabric required
$\frac{5}{8}$ yd single thread tapestry canvas, 27 in wide, 18 threads to 1 in.
Cream fabric for backing, 19 in square.

You will also need
D.M.C. Tapestry Yarn: 43 skeins ecru.
Pillow form to fit.
Tapestry frame with 27 inch sides.
Tapestry needle No. 18.

The design
1 Mark the center of the canvas along a line of holes in both directions with basting stitches. Mount the canvas in the frame, with the raw edges to the tapes. When working fern stitch turn the frame on its side to allow the stitches to be worked in the correct direction, as indicated by the black arrows on the working chart. The working chart gives a section of the complete design. Blank arrows indicate the center of the design, which should coincide with the basting stitches.
2 Follow the working chart using the stitch key for the design. Each background square

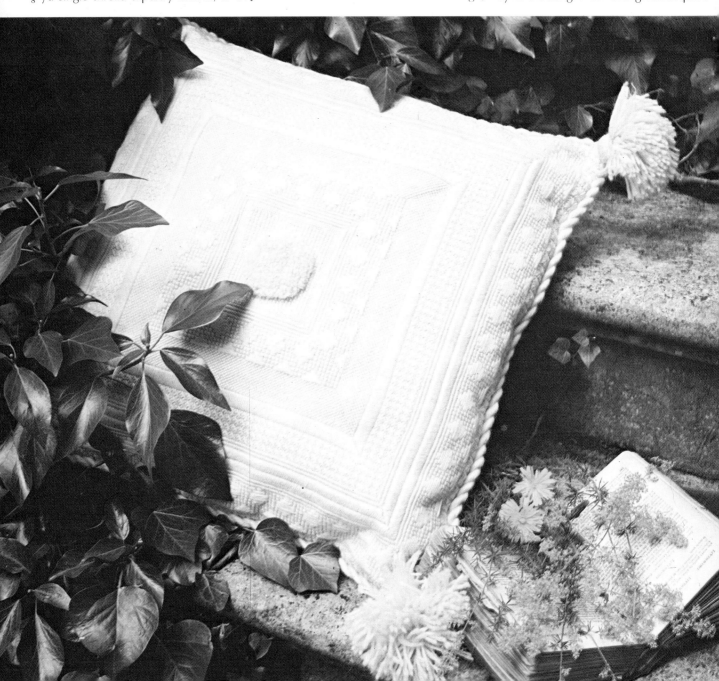

represents two threads of the canvas. Detailed stitch diagrams are given showing the number of threads over which the stitches are worked. When working cross-stitch it is important that the stitches are crossed in the same direction.

3 Begin the design at the small black arrow 6 threads down and 14 threads to the left of the crossed basting stitches in the center of the canvas, and work the section as given on the working chart. Omit the center section and repeat the stitches in reverse from the blank arrow to complete one quarter of the design. Work the other three quarters to correspond.

Finishing

The completed canvaswork should be dampened, pinned with rustless thumb tacks and stretched to the correct shape on a clean dry board and left to dry naturally.

To work velvet stitch

This stitch resembles the pile of an oriental carpet. It is worked from left to right in rows working from the bottom upward. Follow the stitch diagram, bringing the thread out at the arrow and insert the needle at A (2 threads up and 2 threads to the right), then bring it out again at the arrow. Re-insert the needle at A, leaving a loop of thread at the bottom, bring the needle out at B (2 threads down). Insert at C (2 threads up and 2 threads to the left), bringing the needle out again at B in readiness for the next stitch. To maintain a regular length to the loops they can be worked over a thick knitting needle. After all the rows have been worked, cut the loops and trim them evenly, taking care not to trim the tufts too short.

Fig 1

Fig 2

Velvet stitch.

To work brick stitch

This stitch is worked in rows alternately from left to right or from right to left. The first row consists of long and short stitches into which are fitted rows of even satin stitch, giving a "brick" formation. The whole filling must be worked very regularly, making each satin stitch of even length and all exactly parallel.

Brick stitch.

To work cross-stitch and upright cross-stitch

Work the required number of cross-stitches over 4 threads, then work upright cross-stitches between each cross-stitch, working diagonally from the lower right to the top left corner in the following way.
Figure 1 – bring the thread out at the arrow; insert the needle at A (2 threads up), then bring it out at B (2 threads to the left). Continue in this way to the end of the row.
Figure 2 – after completing the last

Fig 1

Fig 2

Fig 3

Cross stitch and upright cross stitch.

stitch, bring the needle through as shown at C. Insert the needle at D (2 threads to the right), and bring it through at E. Continue in this way to the end of the row. Figure 3 shows the finished effect.

To work fern stitch

Pull the thread through at the arrow and insert the needle 2 threads down and 4 threads to the right bringing it out 2 threads to the left. Then insert the needle 2 threads up and 4 threads to the right. Bring it out 2 threads down and 4 threads to the left in readiness for the next stitch. The Chart shows the direction of the two rows of fern stitch as they have been worked on the pillow.

Fern stitch.

To work eye stitch

This stitch is worked in the same way as star stitch to form a square over 8 horizontal and 8 vertical threads of canvas. It consists of 16 straight stitches all taken into the same central hole but with their outer ends arranged over a square of eight threads. Finish the square with an outline of backstitch worked over 2 canvas threads, shown in Figure 2.

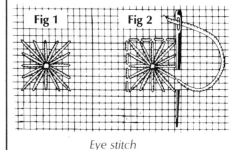

Fig 1   Fig 2

Eye stitch

To work straight gobelin stitch

Work a trammed stitch from left to right, then pull the needle through 1 thread down and 1 thread to the left, inserting again 2

Straight gobelin stitch.

threads above. Pull the needle through 2 threads down and 1 thread to the left in readiness for the next stitch.

To work the cord

Measure off six 15 yard lengths of yarn. With someone to help you, double the pieces of yarn in half to make a length of $7\frac{1}{2}$ yards, then knot the loose ends together and insert a pencil at each end. Pull the threads and, keeping them taut, turn the pencils around in opposite directions following the natural twist of the wool. Continue until the cord is sufficiently tight and begins to curl. Still keeping the cord tight, place another pencil in the center and double the cord over it until both ends meet, making a length of $3\frac{1}{4}$ yards. Next twist the cord in the opposite direction, until it begins to curl naturally. Set the cord by exerting a steady pull at both ends which will cause it to stretch slightly and so retain its twists permanently.

To make the tassels

For one tassel, wind 2 skeins of yarn evenly around a piece of cardboard 3 inches wide. Tie them together with a piece of matching yarn at one end, cut the yarn at the opposite end, and then remove the cardboard. Now take another $\frac{1}{4}$ skein of yarn, and wind this around the tied ends near the top to form a head, then fasten off securely. If the yarn does not lie properly when the tassel is completed, hold it for a few minutes over a steaming kettle, or press with a cool iron.

To finish

Trim the canvas, leaving a 1 inch border of unworked canvas all around. Place the canvaswork and backing fabric right sides together and sew them together close to the embroidery around three sides. Turn back to the right sides, insert the pillow, and slip stitch along the opening. Stitch the cord in position around the edge of the pillow and attach the tassels securely to the corners.

KEY
1 Velvet stitch
2 Cross-stitch
3 Satin stitch
3a Satin stitch (horizontal)
4 Brick stitch
5 Cross-stitch and upright cross-stitch (variation)
6 Fern stitch
7 Eye stitch
☐ Petit point
☐ Straight gobelin stitch

Satin stitch

Petit point

Cross stitch

Chart for pillow

(Each square = 2 stitches)

Quillwork desk set

For your desk

This smart desk set was inspired by the quill work embroidery of North American Indian tribes. The colors – ocher, indigo and rust – are similar to those produced by natural dyes. The embroidery is worked throughout in variations of satin stitch. The simple basic design can easily be adapted to make the pieces of the set larger or smaller if you wish.

Fabric required

$\frac{2}{3}$ yd single thread canvas, 16 threads to 1 in, 23 in wide, $\frac{1}{4}$ yd felt, 72 in wide, to match one of the main colors.

You will also need

Anchor Tapisserie Yarn in the following colors and quantities: 8 skeins 0850 indigo, 7 skeins 0412 rust, 5 skeins 0315 ocher, 4 skeins 0848 light blue.
Hardback address book, 5 in by 8 in.
$10\frac{1}{2}$ oz soup can, 4 in high, for pencil holder.
Piece of heavy cardboard, thin plywood or plastic sheet 16 in by 23 in.
Tapestry needle No. 22.
Sewing needle.
Thread to match felt.

The design

1 Tape the raw edges of the canvas and, following the working charts, work the parts of the desk set. Do not cut the canvas, but leave a 2 inch border of unworked canvas around each piece of embroidery. The embroidery is worked throughout in satin stitch of various lengths.
Note It is important when working the design to remember that each square on the chart represents two stitches.
2 The completed canvaswork should be dampened, then pinned and stretched to the correct shape on a clean dry board, and left to dry naturally.

Pen holder

Trim the unworked canvas to $\frac{3}{4}$ inch all around. Fold the canvas around to form a ring, trim the top layer of unworked canvas down to 4 threads. Work satin stitch, using indigo thread, over the 4 threads as shown, joining the two layers of unworked canvas.
Cut a strip of felt 4 inches by 9 inches and sew the short ends together. Turn under the border of unworked canvas around top and bottom, slip the felt inside the canvas and slip stitch together around top and bottom. Fit the completed cover over the can.

Address book cover

Trim the unworked canvas all around to $\frac{3}{4}$ inch. Miter the corners and fold down the borders of unworked canvas. Cut a

strip of felt 11 inches by $8\frac{1}{4}$ inches. Stitch one short end of the felt to the canvas as shown in the diagram. Cut another piece of felt $4\frac{1}{4}$ inches by $7\frac{1}{4}$ inches; sew this to the remaining three sides of the canvas.
Slide the embroidery onto the front cover of the book, fold the rest of the felt around the book and inside the back cover. Slip stitch at top and bottom.

Blotter

Trim the unworked canvas to $\frac{3}{4}$ inch all around. Cut a piece of felt as shown in the diagram. Turn under the unworked borders of canvas and sew the two embroidered end pieces onto the felt as shown. Lay the board on top of the felt and fold the end pieces around to the front. Fold the excess felt at top and bottom to the back of the board and stitch down. Cut a sheet of blotting paper to size and insert.

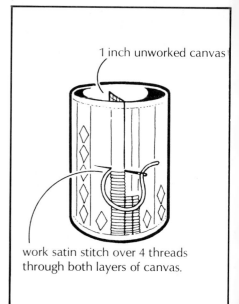

1 inch unworked canvas

work satin stitch over 4 threads through both layers of canvas.

Sewing the pencil holder cover.

felt underneath   sew felt to felt   sew felt to canvas.

felt

Fitting the cover on the address book.   *Cutting felt for the blotter.*

attach embroidery here

16 inches 20 inches

23 inches

3 inches   2 inches

29 inches

Chart for blotter cover

Each square = 2 threads of the canvas

Chart for address book cover

77 threads

254 threads

Design repeats once

124 threads

Chart for pencil cover

63 threads

Design repeats twice

140 threads

41 threads

Anchor Tapisserie Wool

0412 rust
0850 indigo
0315 ochre
0848 light blue

Satin stitch.

FLORENTINE NEEDLEPOINT

Florentine canvas work dates back as far as the 13th century and is thought to be of Hungarian origin.

It is also known as Bargello, which is probably a corruption of Jagiello, the family name of the Polish King Vladislaw who married a young Hungarian princess. She incorporated the arms of Hungary and Poland in a bishop's cope which she worked in the stitch now known as Florentine.

It became known as Florentine work in the 15th century when one of the Medici family married a Hungarian bride who taught the art to the ladies of the Florentine court. Other names for Florentine work include Hungarian point, "Fiamma" or flame stitch.

There is a great difference between the Florentine work of the past and that of today. The main characteristic of the work is the shading and blending of color, but while the early work was subtle with carefully arranged color tints, modern work is bolder and more striking.

Traditionally Florentine work was used for upholstery on stool tops, chair seats and bed drapes, but today it can also be made into stunning accessories, such as the bag shown on the page opposite.

Choosing the colors

As a general rule, it is advisable to use two or three basic colors with as many intermediate shades of these colors as you like. Each successive row is worked in a lighter or darker tint to that of the previous row, so gradually shading from one tone to another. When you are working in shades which are very close, it is advisable to lay all the skeins of yarn on a table and grade them carefully. Number each one with a small tie-on label so that you can always pick up the threads in the correct sequence.

Materials

Use single thread canvas with yarn in the correct thickness to match the mesh and completely cover the canvas. On a 16 or 18 mesh canvas, tapestry and crewel wools (with three strands) are the ones most frequently used because they both have an excellent color range. Knitting wool can also be used and silk threads worked on a fine mesh canvas.

Estimating the amount of yarn

1 Cut a 18 inch length of yarn. Stitch as much of the pattern repeat as this length will allow and then count up the number worked. Multiply by the yarn length to calculate how much you need for a complete row and then multiply that by the number of rows worked in each color.

2 Calculate from the yardage specified by the manufacturer how many skeins of each color you will need.

Needles

Use tapestry needles of a suitable thickness for the canvas and yarn.

Frames

Technically this form of canvas work can be evenly stitched whether held in the hand or mounted in a frame, so whichever method you use is a matter of personal preference.

Preparing the canvas

Baste the center lines both vertically and horizontally on the canvas plus any other guide lines you feel necessary. Count and mark the high points of any pattern where the repeat is the same throughout.

The stitch

Only one type of stitch is used for Florentine work. It is a vertical stitch usually covering an even number of threads, such as four, six or eight, and moving either upward or downward over one or more threads depending on the pattern.

Patterns are constructed by working blocks of stitches side by side, then moving higher or lower to make another block, and so on.

Zig zag stitch

This is the most commonly used Florentine stitch and is worked by passing each stitch over four threads and back under two. The easiest way to vary it is to take it over six threads and back under one. To avoid monotony in the pattern, vary the height

of the pinnacles formed or make the slopes more gradual, perhaps by making two stitches over the same number of threads.

Flame stitch

This is worked over four threads and back under one and produces a flame-like effect. It is important to start in the center of the canvas with the apex of the stitch at the

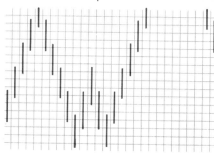

highest point. Both flame stitch and Florentine stitch can be the basis of more complex designs using squares, diamonds or trellises.

Curves

You can form the illusion of a curve by working blocks of stitches over the same

number of threads and varying the rate of progression. Thus stitches or blocks of stitches worked on the 6/1, 5/1 and 4/1 principle will produce steeper curves than those worked on the 6/3 and 4/2 principle.

Medallion pattern

This is a popular repeating pattern where each stitch is taken over four threads and back under two, starting with four single stitches, followed by one block of two stitches, then three blocks of three stitches to form the top of the pattern.

Progress downward, repeating the same number of stitches. This forms the outline of the pattern which can be repeated throughout the work. The spaces formed between the medallions can be filled with contrasting color yarns.

The foundation row

All Florentine patterns depend on an accurate first row and in some patterns the embroidery is worked either above or below this row. In others each section is filled in from one outer foundation row.

When working this foundation row it is extremely important to count the threads accurately – if you make a mistake, cut it out rather than trying to unpick it, since unpicking takes too long and frays the yarn so badly that it is unusable.

Starting and finishing

For patterns where symmetry is important, begin at the marked center line of the canvas and stitch the first row from the center outward. The following rows can be worked from side to side in the usual way, following the pattern established by the first row.

Florentine clutch bag

Use a length of yarn about 15 inches long and knot one end. Thread the needle with the other end and pass the needle through the canvas from the front about 2 inches from the position of the first stitch. Bring the needle up in the position for the first stitch, work several stitches and then cut off the knot, leaving the tail.

Thread the tail through to the back of the canvas and work it in through the back of the stitches. Finish off by working a short length through the stitches on the back in the same way. Always avoid starting and finishing in the same place so that the work will have an even finish and darn in the ends as they occur to avoid matting and tangling on the back of the work.

Size

$7\frac{1}{2}$ in × $11\frac{3}{4}$ in × 2 in.

Fabric required

$\frac{3}{8}$ yd single thread tapestry canvas, 27 in wide, 14 threads to 1 in.
Small skin of suede for back of bag and gussets.
1 felt square, 24 in × 24 in.

You will also need

D.M.C. Tapestry Yarn: 4 skeins Raspberry 7209, 2 skeins each Raspberry 7204, 7205, 7215; 1 skein gray 7618.
D.M.C. 6-Strand Floss: 3 skeins rose pink 819, 2 skeins each white, gray 762. Use six strands throughout.
Tapestry frame with 27 in tapes.
Adhesive.

The design

This design is worked in Florentine canvas embroidery.
The photograph gives a section of the design with the double row of three straight stitches forming the center.

Working the embroidery

1 Mount the canvas into the frame. Mark the center of the canvas widthwise with a

line of basting.
2 Start the embroidery in the center of the canvas with the double row of three straight stitches. Work the motifs on each side and repeat to the sides and above and below to the required size. Grade the colors according to the photograph.
Most stitches are worked over six threads of canvas with some stitches over three threads to complete the design.

Finishing

1 Cut out pieces of suede measuring $8\frac{1}{2}$ inches × $12\frac{3}{4}$ inches for the front; 7 inches × $12\frac{3}{4}$ inches for the back, and two pieces, 3 inches × $14\frac{1}{2}$ inches for the gusset.
2 With right sides together stitch the gusset pieces along their short edges making $\frac{1}{2}$ inch turnings. Press the turnings open with your fingers.
3 With right sides together stitch the Florentine flap to one long edge of the suede back. Press the seam open. Working from the right side top-stitch the suede

close to the seam line.
4 Cut out pieces of felt the same size as the suede for the front and gusset and $12\frac{3}{4}$ inches × 16 inches for the flap and back. Stitch the gusset sections as for the suede.
5 With right sides together, stitch the felt back and flap piece to the Florentine flap as far as the fold line which is $1\frac{1}{2}$ inches from the seam.
Clip across corners, turn through to the right side and press. Clip seam allowance at the fold line.
6 Place the remaining felt pieces onto the wrong side of the corresponding pieces of suede and treat them as one piece.
7 To finish the top edge of the front, fold the turnings under $\frac{1}{2}$ inch, place together and glue them. Top-stitch close to the edge.
8 With right sides together, stitch the front to the gusset, clipping the gusset turning at the corners. Finish the back in the same way. Trim seams and turn right side out. Topstitch the seams through all thicknesses $\frac{1}{4}$ inch from the edge.

Florentine chair seat

The quantities and instructions are given for a dining chair with a larger than average seat slip but they can easily be adapted to fit your own chairs.

Materials required

Clark's Anchor Tapisserie wool: 5 skeins each Tangerine 0311, 0313, 0315, Chestnut 0350, Black 0403, 2 skeins Flame 0334.
$\frac{3}{4}$ yd single thread tapestry canvas, 18 threads to 1 in, 27 in wide.
Tapestry frame (optional).
Tapestry needle No. 18.
Paper for making template of chair seat.
Upholstery tacks, $\frac{3}{8}$ in long.
Tack hammer.
Wood plane (if necessary).

Making the template

1 Remove the seat from the chair, place it onto the paper and draw around.
2 Draw a second line 1 inch outside the

KEY TO DIAGRAM

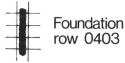

▮	Foundation row 0403
2	- 0311
3	- 0313
4	- 0315
5	- 0350
✛	- 0334

TAPISSERIE WOOL

FLORENTINE STITCH

rst line to allow for the depth of the padding. Draw 1 inch squares in each orner for mitered corners. The stitching hould not be worked in these squares. ut along the outside line.
Pin the template onto the canvas and raw around the edge using a felt-tipped en. Allow at least 1 inch unworked canvas ll around so that it can be attached to he under-side of the seat.

Marking the design
Mark the center of the canvas in both directions with basting.
2 Following the chart, mark the pattern onto the canvas starting at the center (indicated by the arrows) and working outward. Repeat the design until you reach the outside edges.

3 Mount the canvas onto a tapestry frame, if you are using one.

Working the design
1 The design is worked in Florentine stitch and satin stitch over four threads of the canvas. Work the foundation row first in the color shown on the chart, starting at the center and going out to the sides in both directions.
2 Work the next row below the foundation row in the color shown on the chart. The tops of the stitches on this row should be worked into the same holes as the bottom of the stitches on the foundation row.
3 Work all following rows in the same way.
4 When the color sequence is completed,

start again with the foundation row and continue as before, working to the outline shape.
5 To complete the design work the horizontal straight stitches.

Attaching the canvas
1 Place the canvas onto the seat and fold the excess onto the underside. Try the seat in position on the chair.
2 If the canvas is too thick for the seat to fit back into the chair, remove the tacks holding the original fabric. Plane the sides of the frame by the required amount and re-tack the fabric.
3 Miter the corners of the canvas and attach the canvas centrally to the seat as for the cover fabric.
4 Replace the seat on the chair.

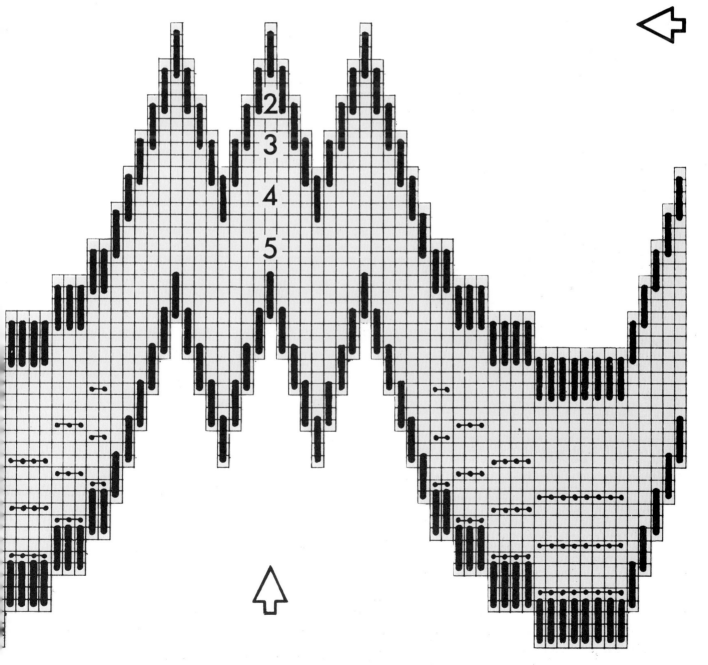

BEADWORK
Simple techniques

Beads have been used as decoration for thousands of years and have been made of many different materials such as pebbles, bone, teeth, seeds, glass and even paper. During the 19th century, embroidery with beads reached its peak when clothes and household articles were often heavily beaded. Berlin woolwork, a form of canvas embroidery incorporating beads, is a good example of this.

Today, beads – wooden, plastic and glass – are used in many ways. They can be combined with stitchery in cut work, needlepoint, smocking, quilting, drawn and pulled fabric embroidery and they can be used without stitchery to decorate any number of things.

Beads

There are wide varieties of beads, sequins and acetate shapes, and they can be obtained in many sizes. Rummage sales and opportunity shops often prove a good source as fragments of old beaded clothes, bags and lampshades will often yield very interesting beads which can be washed and re-used. A bag of "sweepings" from a work-room will often provide sufficient beads and sequins for many pieces of embroidery. When choosing beads for clothes or articles which need to be washed or dry-cleaned, check that they are durable because some acetate shapes will not stand laundering or a hot iron. Most sequins can be washed with care although you should avoid touching them with a hot iron.

Designing with beads

Choose the beads to enhance the background fabric, not necessarily to contrast with it. Often the best effect can be obtained by creating a subtle contrast rather than an obvious one. Always try to avoid crude or over bright effects.

A geometric pattern is probably the easiest way of building up a pattern which can be repeated on a bag, belt or garment, and the simplest starting point is with a square. Start by placing a square bead on a piece of felt and surround it with a row of medium size square or round beads and surround these with a row of flat sequins which might be oval or boat shaped. These could be followed by a small quantity of fine piping cord, securely couched onto the background fabric and covered with succeeding rows of small beads. If you prefer a circular motif, use the same principle but start with a large jewel or circular domed sequin. Another way that beaded and sequinned motifs can be used successfully is to place them on a geometrically patterned fabric, building up a pattern on the design of the fabric.

Whether you decide to build up a geometric pattern or to work out a less formal idea, the design should fill the space intended else it will look thin and meager. Try to insure that different parts of the design balance. A large solid shape should be balanced with several smaller ones. If you are interpreting a design based on cut paper shapes, consider the spaces formed in between the shapes as they are just as important as the shapes themselves.

Frames

It is important to use a square or rectangular frame for bead embroidery. A hoop is not suitable except for an isolated motif since you will often need both hands free and the hoop does not provide sufficient tension on the fabric. When embroidering a section of a garment, mount the whole piece into the frame, complete the bead embroidery, remove from the frame and then finish the garment.

Fabric

Any type of fabric can be enhanced with beads which are suitable for the weight and texture – naturally small glass beads would be unsuitable for a heavy tweed where large wooden or plastic beads would give the best effect.

It is advisable to back the fabric to be embroidered. If it is heavily beaded, a firm non-woven interfacing will support the beads on a bag or a belt. For a garment use a firm lightweight cotton or lawn as a backing for the beaded part only. For this kind of trim, cut away the surplus around the beaded portion before finishing the garment.

Thread

The thread you use will depend on the size and type of fabric and beads. Never use a polyester thread because it stretches too much. The beads should lie on the fabric without being too loose, nor tight enough to pucker it. Pure sewing silk is the most satisfactory thread to use, in a color to match the bead or sequin. Always wax the thread with beeswax to strengthen it and prevent the beads – particularly bugle beads – from cutting into it.

Needles

Use special beading needles which are long and pliable and are available in sizes 12–18. Choose the size to slip through the beads easily.

Attaching beads

Beads, depending on their size, can be attached to fabric in one of four ways.
1 They can be sewn onto the background fabric with a straight stab stitch. The thread is brought through the fabric, the bead is threaded onto the needle and the needle is passed through the fabric again. The bead will then lie on its side.

2 The bead, if large enough, can be secured by two or four stitches through the center hole so that it will then lie with the hole upward. Square beads are more effective when used in this way but the use of this method depends on the effect you are trying to produce.

3 Beads can be sewn on with a backstitch or several beads can be threaded onto a needle and couched down to follow the line of the design.

4 A large bead can be sewn on by bringing the threads through the fabric, sliding on the large beads and then one small matching or contrasting bead. The needle and thread then re-enter the large bead and the fabric. This secures the large bead so that it is free-standing.

It is advisable to fasten the thread off after sewing on each heavy bead, rather than carry the thread on the back of the work from bead to bead.

Attaching sequins

Sequins are available in flat and cupped shapes in a number of sizes. They can be attached as other beads or jewels when used as isolated units or they can be sewn on in line so that they overlap.
1 Bring the needle up through the fabric and through the hole in the center of the first sequin. Pass the needle back through the fabric at the edge of the sequin and bring it up again immediately next to the point that it entered.
2 Thread on the next sequin making sure that cupped sequins all lie in the same direction with the domed side uppermost. Continue in this way along the entire row. Each sequin should evenly overlap the preceding one.

Sewing beads over cord

Piping cord can be used as a base and can be dyed to show through glass beads.
To attach the cord, place it on the line of the design and secure it with three over-cast stitches at each end and with three straight stitches from the fabric to the center of the cord alternately on each side.

To cover the cord with beads, bring up the thread at the side of the cord, slide on enough beads to cover the cord from side to side and insert the needle into the fabric on the opposite side of the cord. Repeat this over the entire length of the cord, keeping the beading tightly packed and with the same number of beads for each stitch.

Attaching bugle beads

Bugle beads can be sewn flat, arranged in regular numbers to produce a repeat pattern. For example three or four beads could be placed vertically followed by the same number placed horizontally; or they could be arranged in blocks such as the brick pattern shown.

Some beads are set in metal mounts which have channels through which the thread passes or they might have a hole in the center or at each end. Both kinds can be attached as for heavy beads.

Fastening on and off

Never use a knot for fastening on or off. Work all ends in securely on the back of the work, keeping it as neat as possible.

A touch of luxury

Add a touch of exclusive luxury to your clothes with this spray motif of beads and paillettes. For a very individual look, beading has been worked here onto the patterned velvet bodice of a smock dress. Tiny pearls and beads in shades of brown and gold subtly pick up the colors of the fabric. Paillettes and a feather stitch trim give the dress an exotic air.

To work the embroidery
Beading is worked more easily in an embroidery hoop. If the beading is to be worked on a garment you are making yourself, do your beading before sewing the seams. Outline the shape of the pattern piece, then position and trace the outline of the motif, either with basting stitches or light chalk lines.

Attaching the beads
On a casual dress which will receive more wear than a special occasion dress, the beads should be attached as securely as possible. Thread used for beading should be the finest and strongest silk or cotton available and should match the background fabric. Use the thread double and draw it across a piece of beeswax for extra strength. Special beading needles, long and very fine, are available in sizes 10–13. To sew the beads on, fasten the thread securely on the underside of the fabric. Bring the beading needle to the front of the work and slide one bead along the needle and onto the thread. Pick up a tiny piece of fabric, the length of the bead along the design line. Draw the needle through the fabric and place the bead in position, then pick up the second bead.

Attaching the paillettes
Use 6-strand floss, either matching or in direct contrast to the color of the paillettes and fabric. The web of stitchery circling the paillette is attractive enough to be a feature of the design. Work with 3 strands of floss in the needle. Hold the paillette in place with your left thumb and take a stitch across it four times (Figure 1). Then make a small stitch over the crossed threads at each of the corners (Figure 2). Place the needle at right angles to the square of thread and pick up a small piece of fabric just outside the edge of the paillette, keeping the thread to the right and under the point of the needle. Draw the thread through, keeping the stitch flat (Figure 3). Still with the thread to the right, push the needle under the thread forming the square and over the thread emerging from the fabric (Figure 4). Repeat the last two steps, working clockwise around the paillette until the circle is complete and the foundation threads covered.

Ideas for using the motif
Work the spray motif as a bold contrast or as a subtle highlight on a dress bodice, a wide waistband, or on the flap of a velvet bag. Try making up your own motif, perhaps one as simple as this arrangement of curving lines. Experiment with simple flowing shapes, placing beads on a scrap of fabric, moving them around and seeing how they look.

Try not to over-bead. A simple motif has impact, while too many beads, especially on a printed fabric, can produce a confused look.

Chart for position of beads and paillettes

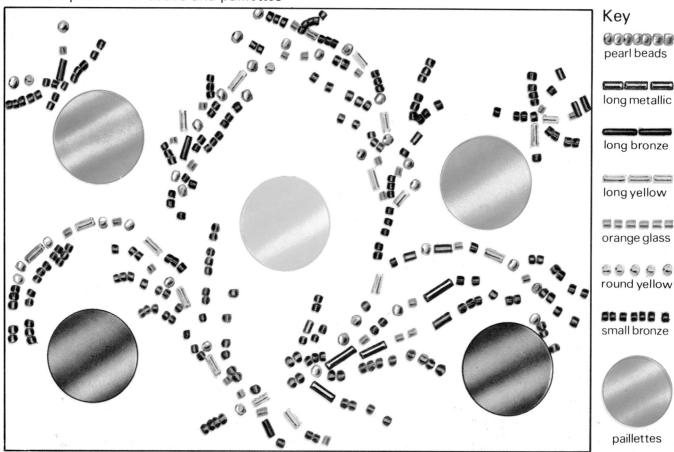

Key
- pearl beads
- long metallic
- long bronze
- long yellow
- orange glass
- round yellow
- small bronze
- paillettes

Other ideas for using the bead motif

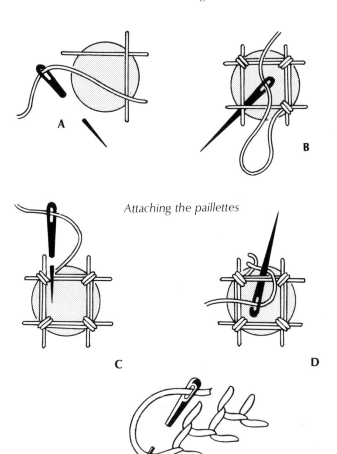

A

B

Attaching the paillettes

C

D

Feather stitch

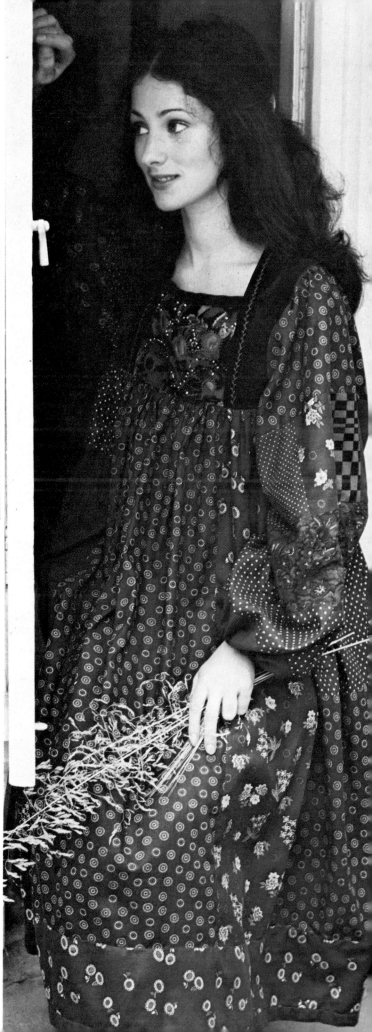

BEAD WEAVING

Bead weaving is an ancient craft used to make a garment, jewelry or a wall decoration. Traditionally it has been associated with South America, where it is often used as a decoration on parts of some national costumes, and where it has developed into a highly decorative and sophisticated art form. Egyptians also used bead weaving and traces of their version of it have been found in tombs dating back 3,000 years.

The equipment
Little equipment is needed for bead weaving other than a beading loom and beading needles. The looms are inexpensive to buy, although you can easily construct one from a wooden or cardboard box by cutting notches along the edge or by hammering tacks along the edge for small pieces of work. The notches or tacks hold the warp threads and the spaces between them should be equal to the length of the beads.

The beads
Any kind of bead can be used, although glass, ceramic, wooden or plastic ones are the easiest to work with. Choose beads of equal size for an even piece of weaving.

Needles and thread
Both the beading needle and the thread must be fine enough to pass twice through the bead. Depending on the size of the beads, pure silk, linen, cotton, or carpet threads can be used. Do not use a synthetic thread, because this tends to stretch. All threads should be waxed with beeswax to strengthen them and allow the beads to slide on easily.

The pattern
The finished bead weaving can be used as a belt, on an evening bag, as cuffs and collar for a dress, or a piece of jewelry such as a bracelet or necklace.
It is easiest to work from a chart, which you can draft out for yourself on graph paper with each square representing one bead of the design. Coloring the chart with ink or crayon in shades to show the colors of the beads makes the chart easy to read while you are working.
A geometric pattern will often produce the most effective pieces of bead weaving, and it is easiest to follow if you intend to build up your own pattern. Alternately, charts for canvas embroidery or cross-stitch can be used and adapted so that one bead represents each stitch marked on the chart.

Setting up the loom
The vertical threads of the design are known as the warp, and these fit into the grooves cut into the combs or bridges on the loom. The beads lie between the warp threads so you must decide how far apart to position the threads and then set up the loom accordingly. There should always be one more warp thread than there are beads in the width of the pattern. To strengthen the weaving when you are using fine threads, make the two outer warp threads double.
To set up the loom:
1 Cut the warp threads to the length of the beading you need plus 6 inches.
2 Knot the warp threads into small equal

bunches, pass them over the roller at the end of the loom and tie them securely to the nail or hook supplied on the roller.
3 Stretch the warp threads tightly across both combs or bridges on the loom, making sure that each warp thread lies in the correct groove. If you are using small beads, the warp threads should lie close together. With larger beads they should be spaced farther apart so that the beads will fit easily between them.
4 Wind the surplus warp thread around the pegs or nails at the opposite end of the loom, making sure that they are evenly taut to give a good tension to the weaving.

Starting to weave
1 Thread the needle with the working thread and attach it securely with a knot to the double thread on the left of the warp threads. If you are using very fine beads, you can give a firm edge to the weaving by working a few rows of darning stitch under and over the warp threads before starting to use the beads.
2 Thread the required number of beads on the needle for the first row of the pattern, working from left to right.
3 Place the string of beads under the warp threads and position each bead between two warp threads. Press the string of beads up between the warp threads with the fingers of your left hand.

4 Bring the needle out around the last warp threads and pass it back from right to left over the warp threads and through the hole of each bead, thus securing the beads in position. Keep the tension as even as possible to avoid distorting the edge of the weaving.

5 Work the remaining rows of the pattern in the same way.

6 When the work is the required length, work a row, or two of darning stitch if you are using fine small beads, and then take the working thread back through the next to the last row of beads and cut the end. Lift the warp threads from the loom and darn each thread back through the beads or in and out of the thread between the beads. Cut the end, making sure you leave no loose ends.

7 If you are making a long length of weaving, work over the warp threads on the loom, then loosen them, wind the weaving around the roller and stretch the unwoven warp threads into the correct position for weaving. Tighten the roller by re-positioning the pin which secures it.

SMOCKING: Basic techniques

No other form of embroidery is quite so simple or so effective as smocking. Through the combined devices of gathering into pleats and subsequent decorative stitching, the appearance of the surface of a fabric and of a whole garment can be changed in the most attractive way.

The history of smocking

The initial purpose of smocking was utilitarian; it was found to be an effective method of controlling fullness in an English laborer's garment. By the 18th century, the popular "smock frock" had become decorative as well as serviceable and, in the next century, this type of garment reached its peak in elaboration. Ultimately the smocked portions of it were combined with a variety of embroidered patterns, the pattern chosen usually depending on the trade of the wearer. This embroidery usually adorned the "box", an area on either side of the smocking, and sometimes the collar and cuffs. Many surviving smocks are identifiable as having belonged to gardeners, shepherds or milkmaids, by the pattern of flowers, staffs, hearts and other similar forms on each.

The designs worked on these hardwearing linen smock frocks were seldom drawn onto the fabric before working, since the needlewomen who worked them had developed a keen eye for following the thread of the fabric. The most frequently used ground fabric was heavy weight linen, often in a natural unbleached color, with the embroidery worked with a twisted linen thread. Both materials were sturdy enough for a garment which had to accommodate activity and ease of movement.

There were no curves at all in the design of the basic smock. It was, instead, entirely a composition of squares and rectangles. One popular style was reversible, with a square opening for the head, and another had a wide embroidered collar. Although all the working in the smocked area was traditionally a variation of stem or outline stitches, a number of other stitches were often used for other decorative embroidery on a garment. Among these stitches were feather stitch, chain stitch, stem stitch, satin stitch and faggot stitch. As in smocking today, the success of these garments depended upon accuracy and even tension of the smocking, as well as a carefully executed choice of stitches.

Smocking today

Over the years, the range of uses for smocking has widened to include an attractive variety of clothes for children and adults. Children's dresses, women's nightgowns, blouses and dresses are all particularly suited to the texture and shape which smocking gives.

Fabric

Among the materials suitable for smocking are linen, cotton, nylon, voile and velvet. Any fabric that can be easily gathered is ideal for this purpose. The garment itself will determine the most suitable weight for the fabric to be used. Be sure to allow adequate width for the smocking – about three times the finished width is a general

Surface honeycomb stitch reduces fullness at waist and upper sleeve.

Gathering the material

Feather stitch.

▲ *Surface honeycomb stitch* ▼ *Crossed diamond stitch*

Outline stitch

Trellis and wave stitch

Cable and double cable stitch

Diamond stitch

rule, although this depends upon the tension and elasticity of the stitches, the weight of the fabric used and the depth of the gathers.

Color possibilities

As the decorative value of smocking does not depend on the color – too much color actually detracts from the effect of the stitching – plan your design with a color scheme that is kept simple. There are three possibilities to consider when smocking: you may use threads in the same color as the background fabric, threads in a contrasting color, or threads of various colors. The effectiveness of matching threads is shown on the blouse illustrated. This pink blouse has a little color introduced with some floral embroidery on the bodice, whereas the smocking itself is merely a part of the textured backdrop.

Thread

It is most important that the thread used for the smocking is suitable for the fabric on which it is being worked. Traditionally, a linen thread was used on linen fabric and cotton thread on cotton or similar fabric. In fact, most kinds of embroidery thread are suitable but, for most work, coton à broder or pearl cotton may be

used in a medium sized crewel or embroidery needle. Always work the smocking before a garment is finished. Mark the area to be smocked with a basting stitch following the thread of the material.

Smocking transfers

Ideally, transfers should not be used for smocking, as they are rarely evenly printed and it is difficult to follow the thread of the fabric. If, however, a smocking transfer is used, the spacings between the dots should be determined by the weight of the fabric (a coarse material requires more widely spaced dots than a fine material). Iron the dots onto the wrong side of the material, aligning them with the weave of the material as accurately as possible. An alternative method of using a transfer is to mark the dots on the fabric with a sharp pencil and ruler. This is, in most cases, a more accurate way of aligning the dots on the fabric.

Gathering up the fabric

To gather up each row, use a strong thread with a secure knot at one end. Begin on the right side of the first row of dots and pick up a few threads at each one. At the end of the row, leave the thread unknotted. Then, after running across the

second row of dots, tie the two loose ends together. Continue in this way, tying each pair of threads together along the left hand side of the work. Remember, too, that when it is worked, smocking is flat on the surface but has a certain amount of bulk underneath.

The gathered lines should be pulled up so that the folds in the fabric become a series of close, parallel tubes. After drawing up all the rows of gathers, turn the fabric over and begin to smock.

Smocking stitches

Feather stitch, honeycomb and similar stitches are a modern innovation in smocking, the early smock frocks having been originally worked only in variations of stem or outline stitch. Most smocking stitches are worked from left to right with two notable exceptions, Vandyke stitch and feather stitches, which are worked from right to left. It is particularly important to remember that the only knot in the stitchery should be at the beginning of the row. Remember, therefore, to have enough thread in the needle at the beginning of a row to complete that row. After completing the work, remove the basting threads and check the elasticity of the stitchery on the garment.

Smocking on heavy fabrics

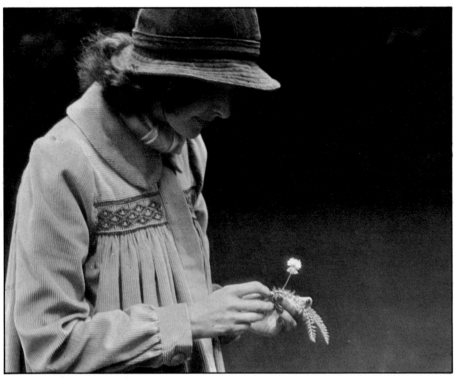

Smocking worked on a heavy cord fabric

Smocking can be just as attractive when worked on heavier fabrics as on traditional fine lawns and cottons.

Many of the same stitches can be used as on lighter materials, although the fabric should be prepared in a slightly different way.

Preparing the fabric

Because of the extra bulk when using heavy fabrics for smocking, allow only twice the required final width before gathering instead of the more usual three widths. If the fabric is dotted, striped or checked, the gathers can be worked using the pattern itself as a guide. If you are working on corduroy the gathers can be worked by picking up alternate ribs, unless it has widely spaced ribs in which case a stitch should be worked on each one. Whether you are buying commercially printed dot transfers or are marking the pattern yourself, be sure that they are fairly widely spaced – approximately $\frac{1}{2}$ inch apart or even more for some of the very heavy fabrics.

If you are unsure, it is advisable to make some trial gathers on a small piece of spare fabric to see how tightly gathered it should be. The fabric should look well pleated and there should be no need to stroke the gathers down as they should lie in flat and even folds.

If you are smocking a definite pattern, count the number of rows and gathers required to complete the pattern accurately, and work the gathering to allow for this. This is particularly important with wide patterns such as open diamond, feather and chevron stitches.

The threads

Use pearl cotton, coton à broder, stranded cotton (use all six strands) or pure silk twist when smocking on heavy fabrics. It is possible to use a fine string or carpet thread on some fabrics such as burlap and linen scrim

The design

Plan the smocking design carefully before you start work as it could be spoiled if a good balance has not been worked out

Figure 1

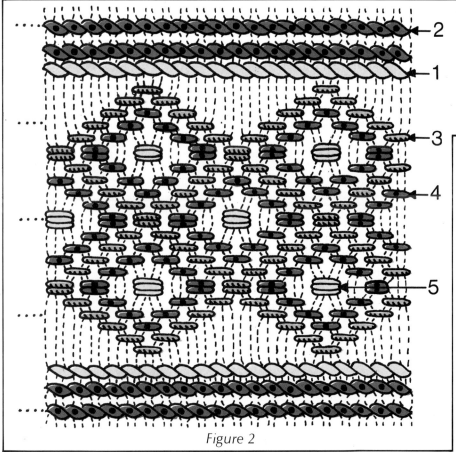

Figure 2

not pull too tightly since the finished garment must have elasticity.

Figure 2 indicates a section of the design repeated across the fabric. The dotted lines at the left hand side indicate the lines of gathers and the placing of stitches in relation to the rows. The vertical broken lines indicate the pleats.

Stem stitch Working from left to right, fasten the thread on the wrong side and bring the needle up through the first pleat. Pick up the top of the next pleat inserting the needle at a slight angle with the thread below the needle. Always work

Key
1 – 0303	**Stem stitch**
2 – 0352	
3 – 0309	**Wave stitch**
4 – 0352	
5 – 0303	**3 straight stitches**

the thread over two pleats but pick up only one (figure 3).

Figure 3

Wave stitch Working from left to right fasten the thread on the wrong side and bring the needle through to the left of the first pleat. Take a stitch through the second pleat on the same level with the thread below the needle, then take a stitch on the third pleat slightly higher than the previous pleat with the thread still below the needle. Continue in this way for five stitches finishing the top stitch with the thread above the needle. This completes the upward slope. Work in the same way on the downward slope except with the thread above the needle (figure 4).

Figure 4

between the various patterns. The basic smocking stitch is stem or outline stitch and this should be used at the beginning of the work along the edges of the border to give it a firm foundation. The modern introductions of feather stitch and herringbone stitch are better used sparingly as they tend to mask the pleated background which is such an important characteristic of smocking.

The pattern shown in the photograph is a simple design using stem stitch and wave stitch and it can easily be adjusted for garments made from heavy fabrics.

Stem stitch and wave stitch pattern

Mark the areas to be embroidered on the wrong side of the pieces to be smocked within the rectangles already marked. Use a soft pencil or tailor's chalk for this and draw fine parallel lines $\frac{1}{2}$ inch apart. Using the horizontal lines as a guide, work five rows of gathering stitches, making sure that the stitches correspond exactly on each line (figure 1). Pick up a small thread only at regular intervals and leave a loose thread at the end of each row.

Pull up the lines of gathering, easing gently to form pleats. Do not pull up too tightly as the pleats must be flexible enough to work the stitches over. Tie the loose ends together in pairs close to the last pleat.

When working the smocking stitches, do

Honeycomb smocked bedspread

Fabric required

Cotton gingham with 1 inch checks. Calculate the amount of fabric you need by measuring the width and length of the bed, allowing $\frac{1}{2}$ inch for turnings and 4 inches for the pillows. Allow the same amount of plain cotton fabric for the backing.

For the ruffle, measure the height of the bed from the floor and to allow for gathering, multiply the length of the bed by 3 and the width by $1\frac{1}{2}$.

You will also need

6–7 skeins 6-strand embroidery floss.
Crewel embroidery needle.
Regular sewing thread.

Finishing this piece

1 Mount each piece of gingham with a plain piece of fabric. Baste all around the edge.

2 Join the pieces for the ruffle, matching the checks of the gingham carefully. Press the turnings open.

Working the smocking

The smocking is different from regular smocking in that the fabric is not gathered first. The stitches are worked on the corners of the gingham squares and form a honeycomb pattern.

1 Working from right to left on the right side of the fabric, leave a complete gingham square along the top and right hand edge of the flounce. Using three strands of embroidery floss, knot the end of the thread and make a small stitch at the bottom right hand corner of the first square.

2 Pass the thread along the front of the fabric and make another small stitch at the bottom right hand corner of the next square. Pull the thread tight, thus drawing the first and second stitches together. Make another half backstitch and pass the needle onto the wrong side of the

fabric. This completes the first honeycomb stitch.

3 Still with the needle on the wrong side, bring it out at the corner of the next square.

4 Keep the fabric flat between the previous stitch and this point and make a small backstitch to secure the thread. Then pass the needle along the front of the fabric and make a small stitch at the corner of the next square.

Pull the thread tight to draw the third and fourth squares together.

5 Continue in this way until six honeycomb stitches have been made.

6 Move to the row below and work five honeycomb stitches in the alternate spaces

to those on the row above so that you are joining the second square to the third, the fourth to the fifth and so on.

7 Work four honeycomb stitches centrally in the third row, thus omitting the first and sixth stitches of the first row.

8 Work three honeycomb stitches in the fourth row, two stitches in the fifth row and one stitch in the sixth row to complete the V shape.

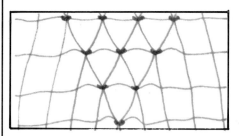

9 Work the next blocks of stitches in the same way all along the length of the flounce. You will now see how the space between the blocks forms an inverted "V" shape.

Attaching the ruffle

1 When all the smocking has been worked, it will form into pleats automatically along the top edge of the ruffle. Pin these down and secure with basting.

2 Make narrow hems along the side edges of the ruffle.

3 Pin the top edge of the ruffle around the edge of the main part of the bedspread and machine stitch taking $\frac{1}{2}$ inch turnings. Make the turnings neat and press them onto the main section.

4 Make a hem along the head edge of the main section.

5 Try the bedspread onto the bed and mark the hem line so that it just clears the floor.

6 Stitch the hem and press the finished bedspread.

Pleated smocked pillow

Sizes

Square pillow: 15 inches square.

Round pillow: 16 inches diameter, 4 inches thick.

Fabric required

For square pillow:
24 in lightweight velvet 48 in wide.

For round pillow:
36 in lightweight velvet 48 in wide.

You will also need

Heavy-duty thread to match velvet.
Graph paper for making pattern.
Basting thread in different colors.
2 button molds, 1 inch in diameter.
Pillow pads in the same size as the finished covers.
Transfer pencil (optional).

The smocking

This sort of smocking is different from conventional smocking. The stitches are all worked on the wrong side of the fabric and do not show on the right side. The fullness is not reduced by gathering, but by drawing points of fabric together to create a decorative pleated finish on the right side.
Although velvet has been used for the pillows in the photograph, this method of smocking is also very attractive on satin or gingham.

The pattern

Each line of smocking is worked over three vertical rows of dots, spaced 1 inch apart. It is possible to buy transfers of the dots which can be ironed on the fabric, but it is quite simple and much less expensive – particularly if you are making several pillows – to draw your own pattern and transfer the dots to the fabric with tailor's tacks. Alternately, you could mark the dots on the pattern with a transfer pencil and then iron it onto the fabric.

Making the pattern

Using graph paper, draw the pattern for the pillow shape you are making to scale. One square = 1 inch. If you are making the square pillow, mark the dots for each line of smocking in different colors as shown so you can easily see where the rows overlap.
Repeat rows two and three until you have ten rows in all.

Cutting out

Cut the fabric in half to make two pieces each 24 inches square. Place the pieces together and pin the pattern centrally to them. Mark the dots with tailor's tacks, using different colored thread for the rows as indicated on the pattern. Unpin the pattern, cut through the tacks and open out the fabric.
Smock each piece separately before making up the pillow.

Working the smocking

To make working easier, the dots are numbered to show the order of the stitches. It may seem very confusing as you start, but after the first few smocked pleats are formed, you will soon find a system.
1 With the wrong side of the fabric facing up, start at dot 1 in the top left hand corner. Using a long length of heavy-duty thread, knot the end and make a small stitch at

dot 2 in the line of dots to the left.

2 Go back to dot 1, make another small stitch over the one already there and then pull dots 1 and 2 together. Knot them tightly by making a loop of the thread above the stitches and passing the needle under the stitches and through the loop. Be careful not to catch the fabric as you do this or the stitch will show on the right side.

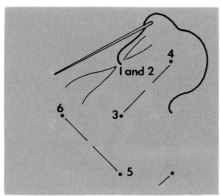

3 Pass the thread along the fabric to dot 3 and make a small stitch. Keep the fabric completely flat between dots 1 and 3, make a loop of the thread above dot 3 and slip the needle under the thread between the dots and above the loop to make another knot. Do not draw up the thread between the dots.

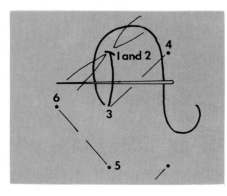

4 Pass the thread along the fabric to dot 4, make a small stitch, go back to dot 3 and make another small stitch. Pull dots 3 and 4 together and knot them as you did for dots 1 and 2.

5 Move down to dot 5 and knot the thread keeping the fabric flat, as at dot 3. Pick up a small stitch at dot 6 and join it to dot 5 in the same way as before.

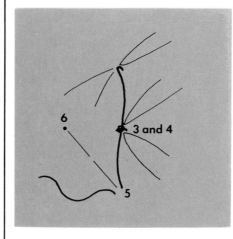

6 Continue down the whole line in this way, picking up a dot on the left, moving down to the next dot in the middle row and then picking up a dot on the right.

7 Work all the lines of smocking in the same way, and then smock the other side of the pillow cover.

Finishing

1 When the smocking is completed, you will find that pleats have formed around all the edges. Pin them down evenly and baste in position, checking that each side of the cover measures 15 inches. Pin the pleats on the other side of the cover in a similar way, having these pleats face the opposite direction so that when the sides of the cover are put together the pleats will match.

2 Place the sides of the cover together, then baste and machine stitch around three sides, making a ½ inch hem.

3 Insert the pillow form, fold under the seam allowance of the opening and slip stitch the folds together.

The round pillow
Cutting out

Cut the fabric in half to make two pieces, 36 inches × 24 inches. Join the pieces along the longer edges, making ½ inch seams and making sure that the pile runs the same way on both pieces. Trim the length of the fabric to 70 inches × 21 inches and use the leftover piece to cover the button molds.

Fold the fabric right side out along the seam line. Place on the pattern with the line indicated to the fold. Mark all the dots with tailor's tacks. Unpin the pattern, cut through the tacks and open out the fabric.

Working the smocking

1 Join the short ends of the fabric, making ½ inch seams. The smocking is then worked in a continuous round.

2 Work the smocking in a similar way as for the square pillow. The finished effect will be less tightly pleated than the square pillow because the lines are spaced farther apart.

Finishing

1 Using strong thread, attach the end securely ¼ inch from the edge of the fabric.

2 Form the nearest pleat with your fingers and make a small stitch through the fold. Draw the thread up tightly.

3 Form the next pleat, take a stitch through

the fold and pull it up to meet the first pleat. Work around the pillow in this way.

4 Insert the pillow form. Repeat on the other side.

5 Sew the covered buttons to the center of each side of the pillow.

Graph for square pillow
1 square = 1 inch

Graph for round pillow
1 square = 1 inch

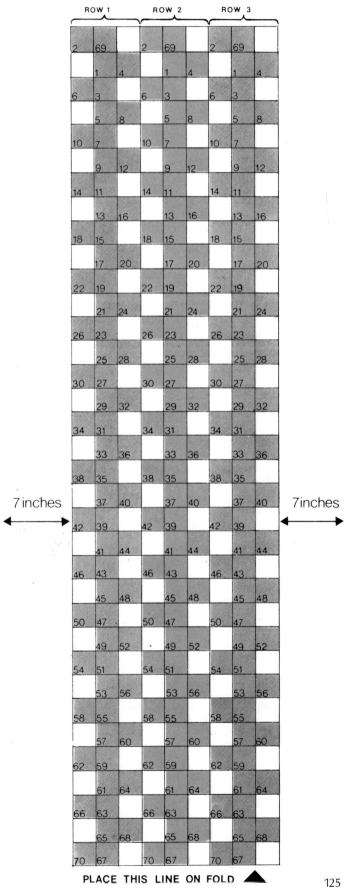

7 inches ←→

7 inches ←→

PLACE THIS LINE ON FOLD ▲

CANDLEWICKING

Candlewick originated in the United States in early Colonial days when, with a severe shortage of sewing materials of all kinds, women settlers used the thick cotton wick intended for candlemaking as an embroidery thread, working it into knotted and tufted designs on bedspreads. For many years the use of candlewick was restricted to bedspreads, but it looks effective in many other forms and can be used for pillows, rugs and bath mats as well as for warm garments such as dressing gowns.

Materials for candlewick

There are two kinds of candlewicking, tufted and smooth, but for both types it is essential that the material on which the embroidery is worked should shrink on the first washing to secure the candlewick in the fabric.

Usually, unbleached muslin is used for candlewick, but linen can also be used.

It is important to choose a weave which will take two thicknesses of the candlewick cotton.

The tracing design given in this chapter is adaptable for almost any use and builds up extremely well, placing the motifs as linking squares. It can be used for both tufted and smooth types of candlewicking and parts of the design might be adapted for a matching border motif.

Yarn

Cotton is used for candlewick and is sold in skeins, available in a variety of colors. Skeins can be cut into 48 inch lengths or, if preferred, wound into a ball and used as desired.

Needles

A special candlewick needle is used. This is a fairly large one with a flattened, curved point and a big eye.

Scissors

It is essential to have scissors which are extremely sharp for cutting the loops. A blunt pair will drag and pull the tufts out of the fabric.

Designs

Designs for candlewick are most effective when based on geometric shapes, but flowing designs can also be used if they are large sized. Small, intricate patterns are difficult to work and the shapes become distorted with the tufting. The candlewick can follow the outlines of the original design, can fill in some areas, or can cover the background completely as an all over design, giving a solid area of pile texture.

Tufted candlewick

In some early examples of candlewick French knots and backstitch were used, but in modern embroidery the stitch mainly used is running stitch worked $\frac{1}{4}$ to $\frac{1}{2}$ inch apart along the line of the design, leaving a small loop between each stitch. To keep the loops at even length place a pencil under the yarn as each loop is made. The candlewick yarn is used double. Cut a length twice as long as is required and thread it through the needle until the ends are even. It is not necessary to finish off the ends when starting or finishing – begin on the right side of the fabric, leaving an end equal to the size of the completed tuft and end in the same way.

When the design is completely worked cut the loops evenly with a very sharp pair of scissors.

Smooth candlewick

This type of candlewick is worked simply in running stitch. One doubled length of yarn is used in the needle as for tufted candlewick and the stitches are worked about $\frac{1}{4}$ inch long and $\frac{1}{4}$ inch apart. This results in a bead-like stitch giving a beautifully raised, sculptured effect. This type of candlewick is at its best worked in geometric designs built up into solid shapes and covering the entire area of the fabric.

Finishing candlewick

The completed work should be washed so that the fabric shrinks to fix the tufts more securely and to fluff them up. If a washing machine is used, wash for at least

A tracing design for working in either tufted or smooth candlewicking

A detail of the design above worked in tufted stitch and showing the reverse side.

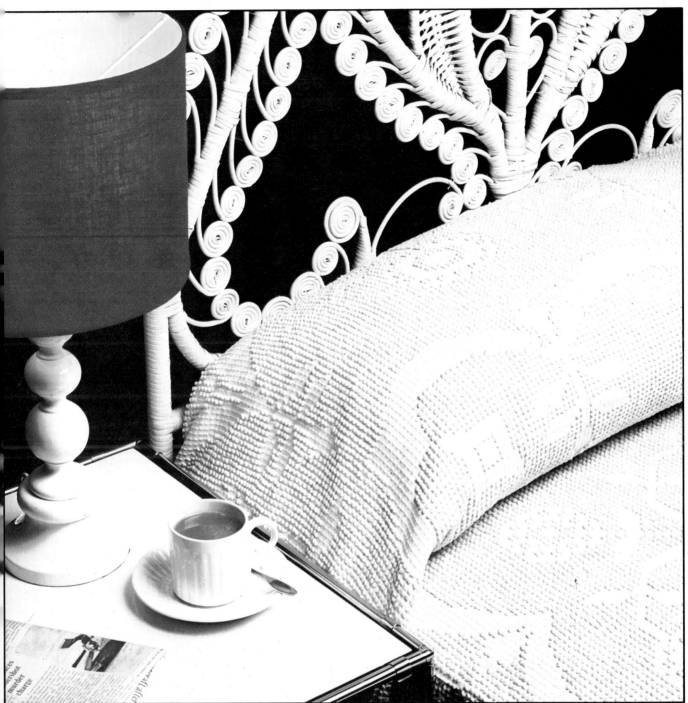

Smooth candlewicking in a modern bedspread.

20 minutes in warm soapy water. If washing by hand let the work soak for three to four hours. Do not wring or squeeze, just shake out.

Dry the work outdoors in a strong breeze and shake it frequently while drying to avoid its creasing and to make the tufts fluffier, then finally brush the tufts lightly with a soft brush before they are quite dry to add further fluff.

It is best to avoid ironing candlewick since this will flatten the tufts again.

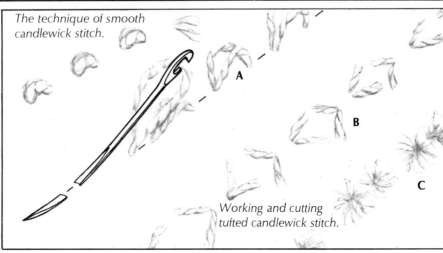

The technique of smooth candlewick stitch.

A

B

C

Working and cutting tufted candlewick stitch.

MACHINE EMBROIDERY
BASIC EQUIPMENT

Although the sewing machine is a standard piece of equipment in so many homes, it is seldom used for embroidery and many people are not even aware of its decorative potential. In these chapters we introduce you to the simpler aspects of machine embroidery and to a whole new range of decorative effects and stitches, many of which can be created with even the simplest straight stitch machine.

Machine embroidery is not only a quick method of decorating clothes and home furnishings. It can be as delicate as traditional hand embroidery or as bold and chunky as a rug or a heavy woven wall hanging. The possibilities are endless. Another important decorative function of the machine is to secure applied fabrics, braids, wool, weaving yarn or even string to the background. In this case the stitching may be nearly invisible or it can be used to supplement the texture of the applied material.

Basic equipment

The only equipment needed for machine embroidery is a sewing machine, fabric, thread, a hoop and tracing paper.

Your machine

It is a common misapprehension that a special sewing machine is needed for machine embroidery. This is not so. There is a great deal you can do on a straight stitch machine and if your machine does even a simple zig-zag you can do a great deal more. The effects that can be achieved with an automatic machine are of course unlimited.

Most modern machines have a drop feed, which is a control to lower the feed for darning and embroidery while others require a plate which will fit over the feed. To adapt a machine, when it is not possible to obtain a plate, the throat plate may be removed and small washers inserted under it before returning the screws. This raises the throat plate to the level of the teeth at their highest point.

Whichever machine you use it is essential that it should be in perfect working order as it receives far more wear during embroidery work than in other sewing, due to the speed at which it is worked. The machine must be cleaned and oiled

regularly. Oil before use rather than after as fine oil tends to evaporate. Run the threaded machine over a spare piece of fabric before starting your work to remove excess oil. Check foot controls and motors occasionally for overheating and should this occur the machine should be serviced.

Fabrics

Many fabrics are suitable for machine embroidery. It is important however that the fabric being worked is firmly woven, so avoid stretch and knitted fabrics such as jersey or crepe which pull out of shape when placed in a hoop. Embroidery will not give with these fabrics. In appliqué work however (described more fully in a later chapter) where the individual shapes are not held in a frame this elasticity is an advantage.

As stitching is so important, and practice is needed to get the fabric into the rings tightly without tearing, the beginner should choose to work on medium weight fabrics such as sailcloth or dress-weight linens. With more experience exciting and varied effects can be achieved using net and fine fabrics such as cotton organdy and even plastic and leather.

Thread

Machine embroidery thread is supplied in two thicknesses, 50 and 30. The 50 is the finer of the two while 30 is comparable in

weight to ordinary machine dressmaking thread. 50 should always be used in the bobbin unless a thicker thread is needed for special effect. 40 and 50 sewing cotton are needed for variety in the weight of stitching and for whip-stitch, while a collection of wool and hand embroidery thread is always useful.

Invisible thread is invaluable to the more experienced embroiderer. It is useful for sewing on fabric pieces when an exact color match cannot be made, and also gives a rich glint to the work when used for free embroidery. It is best used together with machine embroidery thread in the bobbin partly to provide color interest and partly because invisible thread alone will not stand a warm iron. Work using this material should always be pressed from the back.

Glitter threads are also available and handicraft shops will provide a variety of textured threads for appliqué work.

Frames

The hoop comprised of two interlocking rings with an adjustable screw is an essential piece of equipment. An 8 inch to 9 inch hoop is ideal for beginners. The more experienced embroiderer may prefer a 12 inch. A very small hoop is sometimes useful too, for eyelets and working in corners. The most satisfactory hoops are made of wood, are narrow enough in depth to pass under the raised machine needle and have a screw adjustment for extra tightening. Plastic hoops are not as good since they do not grip the fabric as well, particularly if it is a slippery fabric, although covering the inner ring with tape or bias binding may help. Metal hoops have the disadvantage of being too deep to slide easily under the needle on most machines and need complete screw adjustment every time the hoop is moved on the fabric.

Tracing paper

For marking out designs use dressmaker's carbon paper. If the structure of the design is in a straight stitch the main lines may be transferred to the cloth by stitching over the paper with the presser foot down, then tearing the paper away. If the design is heavily drawn on the paper with felt tip pen, it is possible to trace it directly onto the fabric by taping the paper to a window with the fabric over it. Use a tailor's chalk pencil for a dark fabric and a sharp, hard pencil for a light fabric, making a dotted rather than a solid line.

This striking fish design is an example of machine embroidery used to great effect on the place mats shown above.

STITCHES
Automatic stitches

Automatic stitches can be used for a wide variety of very interesting designs. They can be used to good effect with applied pieces of fabric, braid or ribbon, for border patterns and decorative motifs for casual wear, for children's clothes and to give the most ordinary household linens a luxury look. Automatic stitches must be used selectively to achieve best results, for if too many stitches are combined in one design, the results can be confused and unattractive.

Many machines only make stitches based on the side to side throw of the needle, but some combine this with a backward and forward motion of the feed thus affording a much wider range of stitches.

Automatic stitching is normally worked using the press foot in the usual way without placing the fabric in a hoop. Worked freely in the hoop they completely lose their effect unless you have acquired the skill of moving the hoop smoothly with your left hand while operating the stitch lever with your right hand. You can learn this with practice. Free machine embroidery will be described more fully in the following chapter.

The stitching can be done with 30 or 50 machine embroidery thread which gives a smoother and more lustrous effect than sewing cotton or with a thicker thread to give a bolder effect. To prevent the thread from fraying, it is essential that the needle is large enough for the thread to pass easily down the groove and through the eye of the machine. If a very thick thread is used it must be put in the bobbin, a technique which will be more fully described in a later chapter. The stitch to be used should always be tested on spare fabric before you begin your design. The space between the stitches should be adjusted to achieve the desired stitch density according to the thickness of thread.

Some degree of tension is essential on upper and lower threads but swing needle work tends to pull up the fabric more than straight stitching. To counteract this, the upper tension should be slackened as much as possible without affecting the even appearance of the stitching. The lower tension may also be loosened but in

the absence of a numbered dial remember to note the pull of the thread and the position of the screw groove in relation to its socket. In this way the tension may be easily reset for normal sewing. It is often necessary to back the fabric to prevent it from pulling up with the needle swings, or stretching when stitching on the bias. The finer the fabric the more important it is to back it. The ideal backing is vanishing muslin which tears away easily after stitching, although medium weight paper is a good substitute. Pellon should only be used if a permanent stiffness is required. The fabrics should be firmly basted to whatever backing is used.

Automatic patterns need not be limited to straight lines of stitching along the straight grain of the fabric. It is not difficult to follow gently curving lines using the right hand to open and close the stitch width lever to give further variety. It is also possible to put the fabric into an embroidery hoop, replacing the presser foot when the hoop is under the needle. This method is suitable for a series of small shapes or for a design with short lines radiating out from the center. Check that your hoop is small enough in diameter to

pass completely around the needle while resting on the throat plate of your machine. Framing will be described in detail in the following chapter.

The patterns shown may be made even more exciting if shaded threads are used. An interesting effect is sometimes achieved by using different colored threads above and below and tightening the upper tension or loosening the lower tension to give the bobbin stitch colored edges.

The design illustrated above can be worked on most fabrics. It is embroidered in two colors, uses twin needles for the double patterns such as the scallops and a stretch stitch for the heavy lines. The satin stitch is used to stabilize the whole design. Automatic stitches will differ from machine to machine, although similar effects can be achieved on most machines.

This design is worked before the smock is made up. Be sure to cut out the pattern pieces allowing approximately 2 inches all around to make handling easier during embroidery. Allow for extra yardage when buying your fabric. Mark each pattern piece and the design areas with tailor's chalk or basting and work each piece starting at its lowest edge.

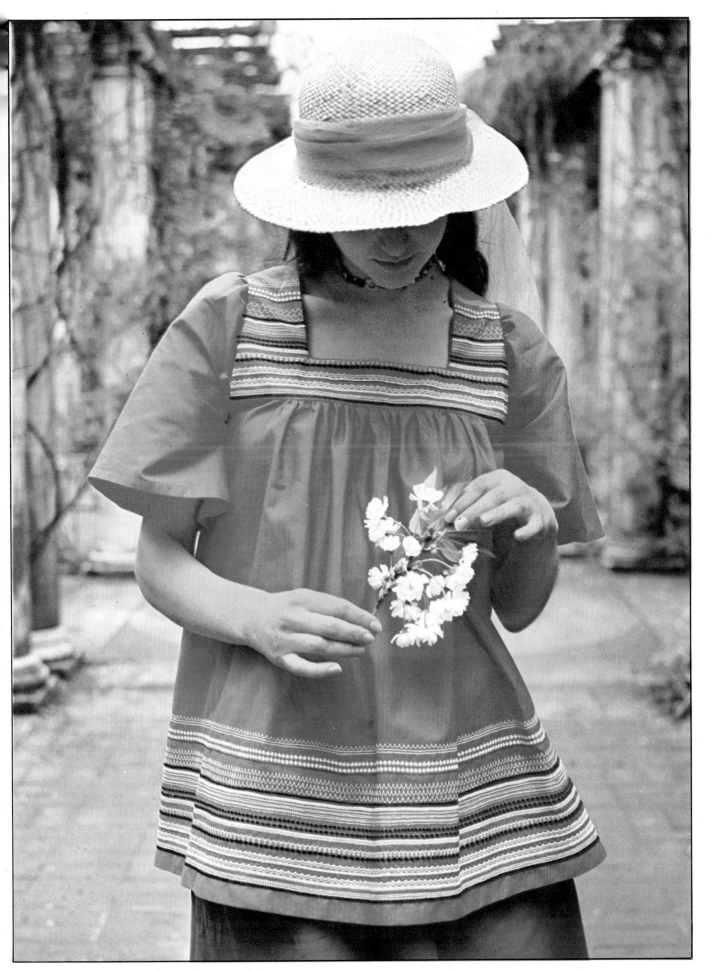

Design using free machine embroidery

It is in free machine embroidery that skill and imagination can come fully into play. The sewing machine is a very sensitive drawing instrument and while mastery of this craft takes practice, it can be very rewarding. Even a beginner can soon produce spontaneous designs of great freshness and originality.

Consult your instruction manual to find out how to convert your machine. If it is an old model, the instructions may come under the heading of darning. The feed will either be covered with a special plate or will be retractable (see earlier).

Framing the embroidery

Frame your work carefully. To do this lay the outer hoop on a flat, level surface, lay your fabric right side up across it and fit the inner hoop into the outer one. The screw should now be adjusted so that relatively heavy pressure is required to do this. Tighten the fabric by pulling it up and in to prevent the rings from dislodging and take care not to distort the threads. If there is any tendency for the fabric to slip back when it is pulled, the screw on the frame should be tightened and the pulling up process repeated until the fabric is stretched to its limit. This cannot be overstressed since the success of all kinds of free stitching depends on careful framing. If the work is loose, it will lift up when the needle passes through it, and the machine will miss stitches which may cause the thread to break. The tautness of the work is the only way in which the tension on the machine thread is counteracted. Badly-stretched work will not lie flat when it is removed from the frame and no amount of steam pressing will help to flatten it. When you are correctly set remove the presser foot and with the needle at its highest point slide the hoop under it. Draw the lower thread up through the fabric and lower the presser foot bar to re-set the tension on the upper thread. The stitch length lever should be set at 0. The size of the stitch is decided by the combination of the speed of the motor with the speed at which you move

the frame. Turn the stitch width lever to 0. Hold the hoop and guide the fabric under the needle. With practice you will find the most comfortable position for your hands. Most of the work is done by the right hand which should swing from the shoulder to move the frame. Control will be greater if your thumb and little finger are outside the frame and the rest of your hand inside, although you must be careful not to get your finger too close to the needle. Place your left hand flat on the work now to hold the work down while you steady it. Bracing your little finger against the edge gives greater control. If the hoop measures 8 inches or less it is probably safer to position both hands on the hoop. Rest your left elbow on the table. The fabric should not lift up while you are stitching, although the larger the frame, the more likely it is to do so.

Hold both threads under your left forefinger while you start, to prevent them from getting pulled down and tangled. Run the machine fairly fast and move the frame smoothly. As a safety precaution do not put your foot on the foot control unit until you are ready to stitch and train yourself to remove it every time you stop. Aim to make 20–30 stitches to 1 inch using a large sharp needle. A fine needle is too flexible and may be broken on the edge of the plate. The needle should take up to a 40 sewing thread; with thicker thread, such as buttonhole twist, you will need the largest needle.

The tension

Although you may not have to alter your tension with some threads, if you use machine embroidery thread for instance, it is wise to loosen the tension by a few numbers. If the thread snaps, loosen it until this no longer happens. If this results in a bad stitch, loosen the lower tension as well. However, you may like the effect you get with a tighter top tension, as the bobbin color will show through to the top. If you do loosen the lower tension, be sure to note the normal pull and adjust the screw only by a quarter turn at a time.

When moving from one part of a hoop to another, raise the needle to its highest point, lift the presser foot bar to release the tension from the needle, move the hoop to the new position, dip the needle down, lower the presser foot bar and continue. If, at the end of a line of stitching, you move your frame slowly to make small stitches which won't unravel, the ends can be cut off close to the work. If the back is to be visible, trim it after you do the front but not quite as closely.

In addition to very careful drawing, you can make interesting filling textures by running the machine at top speed and then moving the frame backward and forward or in a small continuous circular movement. If the machine is set for zigzag, a heavy line can be made by moving the frame slowly. When the frame is moved from side to side with the needle swinging, large stitches can be made up to $\frac{1}{2}$ inch in length. These long stitches catch the light, giving quite a different effect to the same movement done with a straight stitch. Always begin and end satin stitch with a few straight stitches or take the ends through and tie them.

The embroidered cloth

The circular linen tablecloth illustrated is 48 inches in diameter and is divided into 8 sections. The motifs are worked using appliquéd fabric and eyelets (described in a later chapter) and a free running stitch. The design for each section was drawn on paper and basted by hand to the wrong side of the tablecloth. The fabric to be appliquéd was basted to the right side and stitched in position from the wrong side using straight stitch and the presser foot. The excess appliqué fabric was then cut away and satin stitch was used around the edges of the designs. The paper was then torn away and the eyelets and free machining were worked from the right side in the hoop. The edges were trimmed with zigzag stitch, then turned to the wrong side and slip stitched in place. Decorative stitching can later be used on the right side to conceal the hem.

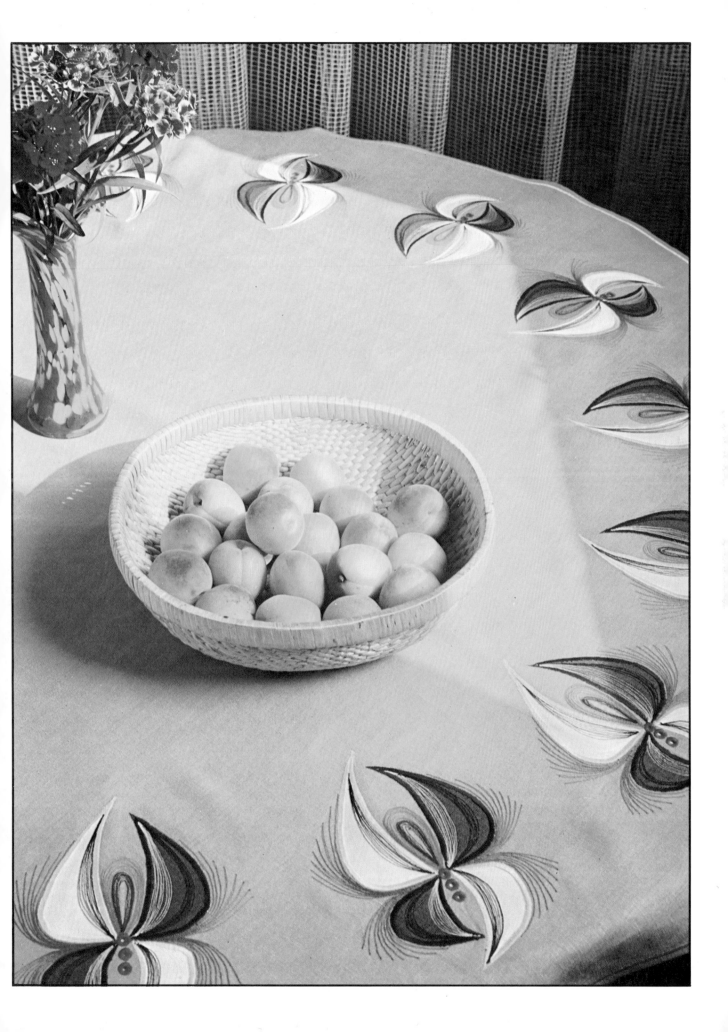

Whip stitch

When embroidering by machine, try to forget all the rules for normal sewing. For it is by using different colors and thicknesses of thread through the needle and through the bobbin and experimenting with different tensions that varied and original effects will be discovered.

One of the most effective variations of the free running stitch is the whip stitch. This stitch lends itself well to small curving designs and looks particularly striking when shaded thread is used in the bobbin. Use 50 machine embroidery thread in the bobbin for best results and a 40 cotton on top. Tighten the upper tension 2 or 3 numbers above normal, run the machine fast and move the frame slowly. If the top thread breaks it may be necessary to loosen both tensions.

The top thread should be flat on the fabric pulling the bobbin thread up. The stitches should be close enough together to enclose the top thread, giving a raised, corded appearance. If the frame is moved quickly so that the stitches are separated the top thread is visible. Different colored upper and lower threads produce a speckled line, but if you move the frame slowly again a solid line will result. A most attractive graded line can be obtained by smoothly increasing and decreasing the speed at which you move the frame. If the upper tension is not tightened enough the top thread will appear at uneven intervals producing a pleasing textural line. Side to side and circular textures are very effective using whip stitch settings.

Whip stitch ends should be taken to the back of the work and fastened, so lines will be continuous wherever possible. If the upper tension is set to its tightest and the lower tension very loose or the bobbin spring completely removed, a feather stitch is obtained. This is because the tight upper tension causes a loop of the bobbin thread to be pulled through to the right side with each stitch. This stitch should be worked in a continuous clockwise or counter clockwise movement. If it is worked in a straight line the result is merely a series of untidy loops.

Remember that whenever the upper tension is slightly tighter than the lower tension, the top color will be affected by the color in the bobbin and, in this way, can be

deliberately deepened or lightened. Experiment by using a range of different colors in the bobbin and by varying the length of the stitches. Whenever you change the direction of the hoop movement there will be a concentration of the bobbin color at the point of change and if you run the machine at full speed and move the hoop in a series of pauses and jerks a dotted texture is obtained. This effect can be used to give tinted edges to filled in designs.

With a tighter upper tension and the needle swinging, a satin stitch with bobbin colored edges is obtained. If the hoop is moved from side to side (full speed essential) in a series of pauses and jerks, crisp satin stitch bars will occur. Do not move the frame until each bar is of the required density.

These bars can be used freely or more formally by stopping the machine after each one to position the hoop accurately for the next. If the needle stops on the wrong side to lead on to the next bar, turn the balance wheel by hand.

These bars could be used to make an attractive decoration for the center of a self covered button or the center of an embroidered flower. Being raised they catch the light and give a rich beaded look although they are best worked with a stitch width of 2 or more.

To avoid unravelling never cut the threads between the bars. You may if you wish, conceal the connecting threads with straight free stitching around the bars.

The panel illustrated is worked entirely in whip stitch using shaded thread on the bobbin and moving the hoop slowly so that the needle thread is concealed.

Cable stitch

Cable stitch is a useful means of introducing heavy lines and textures into a design. It is often used with the presser foot for decorative top stitching but can also be used freely in the hoop. The design is worked from the wrong side. Cable stitch is hard wearing and good for articles which will be in constant use.

With cable stitch the top thread is passed around the thick thread with each stitch protecting it from the rubbing it receives if the thread is applied by stitching along its length.

The thick thread must be wound on the bobbin either by hand or on the bobbin winder. You should create slight tension with your fingers to insure that the thread winds evenly. The thread should be smooth enough not to clog the tension spring. The tension should always be loose so that the pull of the thread feels the same as for normal sewing and the stitch appears even. If you are embroidering an article which will receive a lot of wear use 30 machine embroidery thread or ordinary sewing thread on top. Should you have difficulty getting the thick thread through the fabric when you dip the needle, pierce a hole with a blunt-ended needle. Some machines have a separate bobbin case and the tension screw and spring may be completely removed. Without the tension spring, threads the thickness of soft hand embroidery cotton can also be used. Textured yarns can be used provided they are fine enough to pass easily through the hole in the side of the bobbin case. If you have removed the spring be sure you insert the end into the slot in the bobbin case before putting the screw back.

It is a good idea to wind several bobbins at once if you are working a lot of cable stitches since the thick thread runs out quickly. If the bobbin color is being changed frequently you should change the top thread as well so that the shape of each color area can be seen on the wrong side (the side from which you are working). In this way you can produce very rich and varied textures. If the lower tension is released completely and you are using a fairly fine thread it will tend to be released very quickly from the bobbin, this making a pleasing, textural looped line.

Unless you are completely familiar with the way your machine works, be sure to always work a test sample first. Set the upper tension just tight enough to grip the heavy thread firmly. If it is very tight it can pull a fine to medium thickness thread through a loosely woven fabric to the wrong side, giving a moss-like texture which can be used on the right side by reversing your fabric.

With some machines it is possible to get an effect similar to heavy whip stitch by greatly increasing the lower tension and moving the hoop slowly so that the bobbin thread is encased by the top thread. Even if you cannot manage entirely to conceal the thick thread, this is a very interesting way of working the more solid areas of a design and it looks particularly effective if shaded thread is used on top.

Cable stitching and its variations are especially useful for dress embroidery, since these designs may be marked on the wrong side. When the cable stitching is completed it should give enough guidance for free stitching or other work on the right side, without any further mark needed.

The sample shows a freely drawn motif worked in cable stitch and free running stitch. To achieve the bobbled effect on the cable stitch, the tension screw and spring on the bobbin are completely removed. Silky hand embroidery thread is used on the bobbin and sewing thread through the needle. For the free running stitch, machine embroidery thread is used on the bobbin and through the needle. This stitch is worked after the cable stitch from the right side.

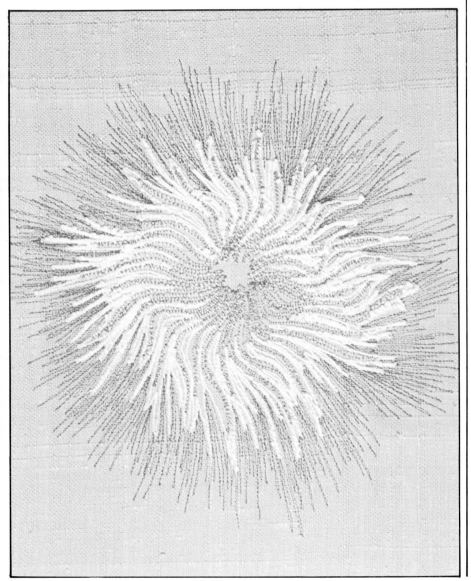

DECORATIVE EFFECTS
Shapes and appliqué

Decorative effects using the presser foot and satin stitch

With a little imagination decorative effects can be worked with the presser foot, without using a hoop. Lines and sharp angles are easily incorporated. Sharp curves are more difficult to make but can be done more easily with the use of the quilting foot with its shorter length, rather than the presser foot, and the shorter than normal stitch length. Geometric designs should be marked out with a series of pencil dots which show on a dark or a light fabric. With more experience you will also be able to stitch straight between dots spaced further apart. Because the threads at each end of a line should be taken through to the back and tied, lines should be continuous wherever possible. Straight stitch effects can be worked on a reasonably firm fabric without a backing.

Heavier effects can be achieved by working a zigzag or satin stitch over an applied thread. There may also be a special hole through the embroidery foot to guide a fine thread under the needle. An Elna foot is designed to apply any number of threads the thickness of pearl cotton side by side which can be held down with the serpentine (multiple zigzag) or other automatic stitch. This foot can be used on some other machines. On a straight stitch machine it is possible with practice to guide a thick thread under the needle so that it is stitched accurately down the center. These suggestions can be used in conjunction with applied braids and ribbons for border patterns too. If using these the ends of ribbons and braids should have their edges turned in unless they go to the edge of the fabric or are enclosed in a seam. Heavy threads must be passed to the back. When a shape rather than a line is to be worked it is wise to take the thread through the back of the fabric before starting to stitch. This will prevent the thread from obscuring your work as you sew and also will help to prevent tangling. Always work the heaviest stitching in a

design first, thus forming the main structure to which finer straight stitching or free machine embroidery may be added. On a fully automatic machine the stretch stitch makes a heavy line which can be used decoratively on the right side of the fabric. The twin needle can be used to make freely shaped pin-tucks either on the background fabric or on fabric to be applied. If a transparent fabric is used a colored wool or embroidery thread can be laid under the needle to give a shadowed effect. Buttonhole twist can be used through the needle (largest size for your machine) to give a thick line on the right side, although thicker threads must be used in the bobbin and the lower tension should be released until it feels the same as for normal sewing. The work must be wrong side uppermost. This is called cable stitch and was described in an earlier chapter.

Always work a sample on the fabric to be used to check tension and stitch length. Only use closely woven fabric or the satin stitch will have irregular edges. Work with tensions as light as possible and take care there is no weight on the fabric passing under the foot which might distort the fabric. If any pulling up of fabric occurs either back the fabric with a thin fabric or stretch the work in a hoop. If a lengthening of the stitch is required as well as variation of width this is best achieved by pulling the work gently through the machine. It is not possible to alter both stitch width and length at the same time. Ends should be taken through to the back and tied.

The panel is worked in satin stitch using the presser foot. 50 machine embroidery thread in shaded colors is used throughout. The area of each square in the design is marked on the background with light pencil dots and the shapes are filled in from the outside toward the center.

Place mats

These place mats were illustrated in the first chapter in this section. They are made of washable linen and heavy cotton fabric. The fish design is worked before the mats are cut out.

The heavy line, designed to be continuous wherever possible, is marked on paper, transferred to the fabric and worked by applying a medium weight embroidery thread with a zigzag stitch and the presser foot. 50 machine embroidery thread is used on the bobbin and through the needle. The design is then placed in a hoop and free machining is worked in different colors to build up areas of texture. The fringed edges of the mats are finished with a machine hemming stitch.

Fine fabrics and nets

One of the great attractions of machine embroidery is that intricate and delicate designs may be completed in a comparatively short time. To achieve anything as complex by hand would take many hours of laborious work.

With a little experience it is possible to place very fine fabrics in a hoop and embroider them although great care must be taken when stretching them in the hoop, since the tension necessary for good results could easily cause the fabric to split. To avoid this adjust the screw on the frame until it is just tight enough to grip the fabric, or tighten the screw and gently pull up the fabric, making sure that you grip it along the width of both palms, spreading the strain as evenly as possible. This needs a lot of patience for if you pull up the fabric between thumb and forefingers it will almost certainly split.

Cotton organdy is a particularly attractive fabric to embroider although it creases easily. It is best used in a design where it will be covered with embroidery. Subtle effects may be obtained by applying pieces of organdy to an organdy background or by placing colored fabric on the wrong side of the background for a shadow effect. Embroidered place mats are particularly lovely when worked on cotton organdy.

Fine fabrics such as organza, cotton organdy or chiffon can be applied to net for evening dresses, or wedding dresses and veils. The fabric to be applied can be mounted on the net and then framed together and tightened securely.

Using free running stitch, outline the edges of all the shapes two or three times. Pull the work clear of the machine, cut away the excess applied fabric and finish the raw edges with further lines of stitching or some fine texture. The shapes should be worked far enough apart to be able to insert the points of the scissors between them.

If the shapes to be applied are very small they may be cut out separately, laid in position and held with the fingers while they are stitched. With more experience you will not be afraid of putting your fingers close to the needle and it is a great advantage to be able to do so. This method is easier to work and there is no danger of damaging the net during the cutting away process. If you are applying pieces of net to net use the second method whatever the size although if the shapes

are very large the presser foot should be used.

Do not attempt to do anything other than straight stitch techniques on fragile fabrics. Satin stitch may pull up the fabric so that it is not possible to press your work flat and also fine threads may get dislodged spoiling the effect of the stitch unless its purpose is purely textural.

Embroidery worked on an open fabric gives a completely different effect to that worked on a closely woven fabric since with an open fabric both upper and lower threads are visible so the stitching appears heavier. All weights of net can be embroidered from the heavy net used for ballet tutus to a fine dress net. Shapes may be embroidered on net then cut out and applied to, or inserted into, another fabric. If you are applying net shapes to a solid background either turn the edges under, making a clearly defined edge which can be secured with hemming or zigzag stitch. Alternatively you could leave $\frac{1}{2}$ inch outside the stitching on each shape and attach it with free machine embroidery which will soften the edge and blend it into the background. This method of machine embroidery is very good for decorating clothes since the minimal amount of stitching needed on the background will not impair its draping qualities. Use soft dress net for the embroidered shapes which may be applied with some other shapes in a more closely woven fabric for contrast, overlapping the net shapes on the others for even greater variety.

Use your imagination when choosing your background fabric. Plastic mesh vegetable bags can make interesting backgrounds for panels. Satin stitch can be used but generally straight running stitch is most effective used in a very textural way with contrasting bobbin colors to build up subtle shaded areas. Some cotton vegetable bags have a very open weave and, once washed, are excellent to use. The threads can be dislodged to make large holes and spaces to contrast with heavily worked areas. They are ideal for lampshades when mounted over a fabric fine enough to allow the light to pass through.

The motif illustrated is worked in the frame. The organdy shapes are applied to the background with free running stitch using 50 machine embroidery thread on the bobbin and through the needle. The edges of each shape are trimmed after stitching and emphasized with more running stitch. An eyelet is worked in the center of the motif (see the following chapter), and a free running texture worked around it. The leaves are worked in free running stitch with sewing cotton.

The delicate art of eyelet embroidery and openwork

Eyelets are simple to work and extremely effective when used on their own, or in combination with other free stitching effects and they always make an interesting focal point in a design. The machine attachments for eyelets are "extras" and are usually made in two or three sizes. When working eyelets, the smaller you make your central hole, the wider your stitching can be and vice versa.

The work must be placed in a hoop using a hoop small enough to revolve around the needle completely and the eyelets should be positioned within the frame so that they do not hamper this movement. Follow the machine manufacturer's instructions for fitting the eyelet plate. For best results use 50 machine embroidery thread. When piercing the hole using the awl supplied with the attachment, be careful not to make the hole too large. Set your machine for satin stitch, place the work in position on the eyelet plate, (you may have to remove and replace the needle), position the needle to the left and draw the thread up through the hole. Hold both thread ends when starting and run the machine fast revolving the frame evenly. It is better to turn the frame twice quickly rather than once slowly, although a delicate effect can be achieved by spacing the stitches so that the fabric remains visible between them.

When the eyelet is completed the ends of the stitching should be tied on the wrong side of the fabric. If a number of eyelets are to be worked this can be avoided by having the eyelets touch each other or else designing the work so that the linking threads may be concealed by further textural stitching. Another way of finishing is to position the needle to the right and work another row of small straight stitching around the circumference of the eyelet. The threads can then be cut close to the work and the stitching gives an added finish.

A further textural variation can be given to eyelets by working through the needle with a different color from that on the bobbin and with the upper tension tighter than the lower so that the bobbin color shows around the edges. Loosen the lower tension as well if necessary.

Openwork may be described as a decorative version of darning. It is the technique either of inserting a delicate web-like pattern of machine stitching into specially prepared holes and spaces or working over the spaces so solidly that they become as heavy as the background fabric. If this technique is to be used for dress embroidery the shapes should be well filled if they are large. If the shapes are small, however, they may be left more open but are best worked where there is no likelihood of damage from such things as buckles, handbags or bracelets.

Generally with openwork the same thickness of thread is used through the needle and on the bobbin. It is always important to use a thread that will stand up to wash and wear and therefore choose a thread thicker than 50 machine embroidery cotton. Cable stitch is a good choice of stitch to work as it fills in the space quickly. The tensions for this should always be set as for normal sewing.

For best results use a closely woven fabric of any weight such as linen, sailcloth, cotton lawn or organdy. Place the work in a hoop and outline the shapes with three or four lines of free running stitch which

lie either on top of each other or touching. This will prevent the edges of the shape from stretching. Remove the work from the machine and cut out the shapes close to the stitching. Work a few stitches around the edge to secure the threads, then stitch backward and forward across the space carrying the stitching around the edge to the next line if necessary until a framework has been made. The focal points may then be built up by stitching continuously around any area where lines intersect without necessarily continuing the stitching to the edge. If you change colors during your design either secure the ends by close stitching or else take them through to the wrong side and tie them.

The edges of the hole may be finished with satin stitch, either freely if you are sufficiently skilled or else using the presser foot. Whichever method you use the work should remain stretched in a hoop small enough to pass easily around the needle. A softer edge is obtained by working a whipstitch or free running texture over the edge of the hole which blends it into the background. It is a good idea on a swing needle machine to use a throat plate with a needle hole rather than a slit. If it is necessary to move the hoop on the work to complete your design do not let the edge of the hoop cross the stitching if possible. If this cannot be avoided see that the main bulk of stitching is at right angles to the edge of the frame to minimize the risk of damage and tighten the work from the opposite side.

For purely decorative designs, such as wall hangings and panels, holes of any size up to the size of the frame can be filled. The holes should be rounded rather than crescent shaped as the lack of edge tension on the latter causes too many difficulties in working.

Openwork can look particularly exciting if different fabrics such as leather, foil or metallic material are laid underneath the shapes but you should bear in mind the function of the finished article.

For permanent objects such as mobiles, lampshade rings or millinery wire may be used to give the edges of the shape support. Millinery wire should be cut long enough to go around the circumference twice with the ends touching each other. Conceal the join with thread tied over it. To secure each line of stitching as you work wired shapes, you should stop your machine each time you reach the wire and work four stitches backward and forward over it, (finishing the fourth stitch inside), turning the balance wheel by hand. You should also try to make the basic structure of wide angles to prevent the threads of

your embroidery from slipping. To also help avoid this, it is a good idea, having completed a horizontal line of stitching in your shape, to work the fourth stitch over the wire so that the stitch finishes inside the wire and above that line of embroidery. This means that when you work the vertical line, the first stitch is worked over the horizontal line thus pulling the stitches over the wire close together, helping to anchor them. Satin stitch can also be worked over the wire or ring to conceal it, using the widest needle throw to lessen the risk of the needle catching on the wire and breaking. Shapes may be worked on stiff wire, which can be bent into more complex shapes. To join the wire, cross the ends and wind an elastic band around them. When the shape is completed it can be laid in position on a background and fastened with a few running stitches inside the wire at each point. Then cut the wire at intervals, carefully remove each section, and further strengthen the points of the shape with stitching or conceal them with satin stitch or applied thread. Never cut the loops which result when the wire is removed.

Several of these shapes can make a pleasing arrangement for a panel but should only be used when the completed work will be stretched, or the effect will be lost. This particular aspect of openwork therefore is unsuitable for dress embroidery.

The sample shows a motif worked with eyelets and a variation of whip stitch. 40 sewing thread is used through the needle and 50 machine embroidery cotton on the bobbin throughout.

Embroidered dress

The dress illustrated has the embroidery worked on the front bodice. This should always be completed before the dress is finished. When you cut out the front bodice piece make sure you allow extra fabric all around to enable you to hoop your work.

The free shapes are worked in the hoop using running and cable stitches. Because you are working across spaces the cable stitch can be worked from the right side. Pure silk thread is used through the needle throughout and silky hand embroidery thread is wound on the bobbin. A free running texture is used around the edge of the shape to conceal the raw edges and soften them into the background.

The front bodice is cut out in lining and basted in position on the wrong side of the front bodice, matching notches. The pattern piece is then treated as one layer during finishing.

QUILTING
Basic techniques

From the small fragments found in early Egyptian tombs, quilting is known to have been used as a means of padding garments and bed covers for warmth and as decoration from the very earliest days. Later, quilting was worn instead of armor in battle and it was also worn under metal armor to prevent chafing.

As well as for bed covers and household furnishings, quilting of garments of all kinds for warmth and decoration was universal during the 16th and mid 19th centuries. In the 19th century, when decorative .sewing was at its height, quilting was as popular as patchwork and the two crafts became closely allied. In America, where the latter was an economy measure with the early settlers, it was customary to make patchwork quilt tops during the winter and hold a neighborhood quilting party in the spring to complete the quilts. The two crafts progressed together in this way to an equal degree of technical expertise.

Types of quilting

Today four different types of quilting are practiced in embroidery. These are English quilting, Italian quilting, Trapunto quilting and the delicate shadow quilting.

Of these, English quilting is the most popular and is the only one which provides real extra warmth since it incorporates all-over padding, although the other methods also give added weight and substance to fabrics as well as decoration. All four methods can be used for bedcovers, quilts, pillow tops, tea and coffee pot covers, jackets, housecoats and other similar garments.

English quilting

This is the method of sandwiching padding between a top cover and muslin backing or fabric lining and then securing the three layers together by over-all running stitching. The decoration comes from the patterns worked by the stitching and the attractive texture produced.

Quilting in Britain is particularly associated with North West England and South Wales, and many of the designs have local names, such as the Welsh heart and Weardale chain. Most of them are based on simple motifs of leaves, feathers, circles, scissors, spectacles, and so forth, and it is worth obtaining templates of these basic shapes which can be increased or reduced in size according to the size of the article being made.

Alternatively, some designs used on Continental ceramic tiles might lend ideas for patterns. When planning the design for a piece of English quilting, the pattern should traditionally consist of principal motifs and a background filling pattern which throws into relief the main areas of the design. The filling pattern can be a lattice of squares or diamonds or a series of lozenge shapes.

Italian quilting

This is worked through two thicknesses of fabric only, a top cover and a muslin or lawn backing. The stitching is worked in double lines, $\frac{1}{4}$ inch – $\frac{3}{8}$ inch apart to form channels which are threaded with soft wool, known as quilting 'wool, to give a raised design on the front of the work.

The designs for Italian quilting should be linear and preferably continuous. The scroll patterns on wrought-iron work and the interlaced forms of Celtic decorative lettering are often suitable as the basis for designs.

Trapunto quilting

This is also worked on a top fabric and muslin backing but differs from Italian quilting in that the stitching is worked in single lines which completely encircle shapes which are then raised by padding them with a stuffing of soft wool or wadding.

Shadow quilting

This is a variation of both Italian and Trapunto quilting. The stitching is worked on a transparent fabric such as organdy or organza with a backing of a similar fabric

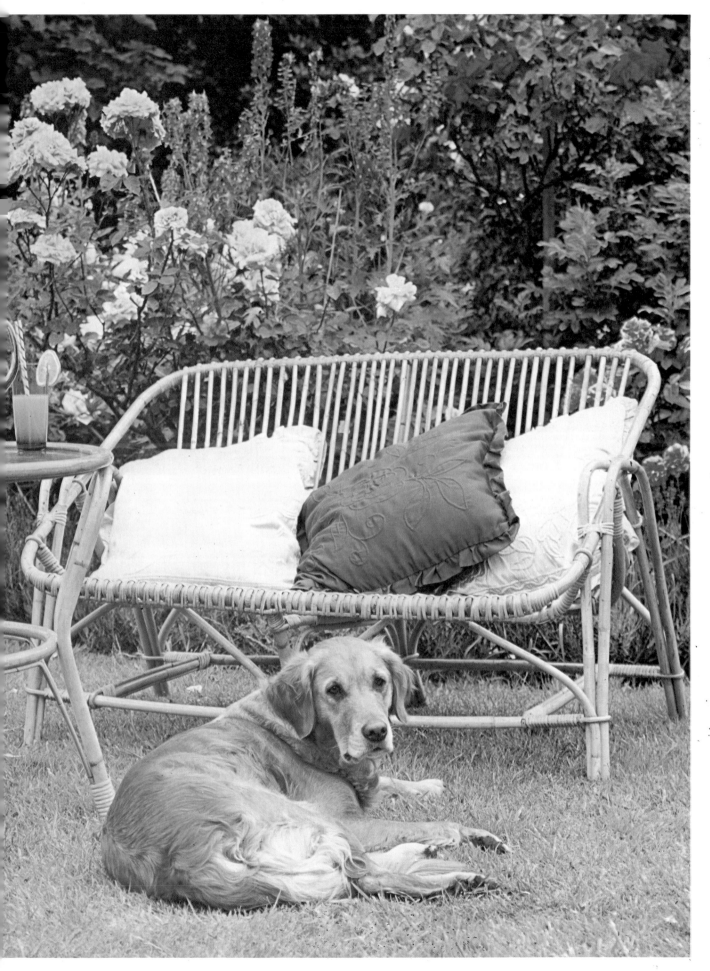

or muslin. The areas to be raised are stuffed and threaded with a colored quilting yarn or soft thick knitting wool.

Fabrics for all quilting

Because it is the design which is all-important in quilting rather than the stitches which are worked in a color to match the fabric, the top cover fabric should be one which really shows the texture formed. For this reason, if you are using satin, it should be the dull sort rather than the shiny surfaced one. Other suitable fabrics are fine silk, shantung, rayon, glazed cotton, fine wool, Viyella, cotton poplin and closely woven linen.

Thread and needles

Pure silk thread in a color to match the fabric is the most satisfactory, although cotton or fine linen thread can be used. For stitching use a No.7, 8, or 9 betweens needle, according to the weight of the fabric. For marking the design for English quilting, you will also need a yarn or rug needle. For threading the quilting wool in Italian quilting, you will need a large blunt tapestry needle.

The stitches

Running stitch is used for all methods of quilting except corded, where herringbone stitch is used.

Working English quilting

In the past carded sheep's wool or cotton wadding was used for padding, but today it is best to use Dacron or other polyester wadding since these can be washed easily (cotton wadding tends to become lumpy with wear and washing). The backing fabric can be muslin or soft cotton if you are lining the article separately, or a rayon lining fabric if a separate lining is not required.

1 Baste the layers together, sandwiching the padding between the top fabric and backing. Work a line of basting across the center of the fabric in both directions.

2 Mount the triple layer of fabric onto a traditional frame, with top fabric facing up.

3 Cut a template of the principal motif, keeping its size in proportion to the article. Place in position on the fabric, using the center basting lines as a guide.

4 To transfer the design to the fabric, mark around the edge of the template with a large needle held at an angle to the work. The point of the needle will leave an impression on the fabric which is easy to follow with running stitch.

5 Work the main areas of the design first in even running stitch. Start the stitching with a small knot on the back of the work which will bury itself in the wadding and finish with a small backstitch.

6 When the main areas have been worked, mark the filling background pattern with a flat ruler and yarn needle. Work along the lines in running stitch.

7 When all the quilting has been worked, take the piece off the frame and finish the article as desired. If you are making something like a bed cover or quilt, one of the best finishes is a piping in the same fabric as the top cover.

8 To attach the piping, make up the casing and enclose the cord in the standard way.

9 If you are using a separate rip out, attach the piping around the edges of the article on the right side and stitch through all layers. Cut the lining fabric to the required size and place it on the quilting with right sides together and edges matching. Stitch along the piping line, leaving an opening on one side. Turn right side out and close the opening with neat slip-stitching.

10 If the lining is not separate, un-do the basting joining the layers together and stitch the piping to the top cover and wadding only. Turn under the edges of the lining and slip-stitch neatly to the piping line.

Working Italian quilting

Traditionally the design was marked on the muslin backing and the stitching worked on this side. However, you may find it easier to keep the running stitches even if you work on the top fabric, in which case the design should be marked by the prick and pounce method (see earlier) and not by tracing or drawing which would still show when the work is finished.

1 Baste the fabric and backing around the edges and mount them as one onto a frame, with the working side facing up.

2 Trace your design onto the fabric and work along the double lines in running stitch. If you like, some parts of the design can be emphasized by working in chain or back stitch on the right side of the fabric instead of running stitch.

3 Thread a large blunt needle with the quilting yarn and insert it along the channels formed by the double lines of stitching. Where there is an angle, break or inter-section in the design, bring the yarn to the surface on the muslin and reinsert the needle leaving a small loop. This allows for an even tension and only a small amount of shrinkage if the quilting is washed or dry cleaned.

Working Trapunto quilting

This is worked in a similar way to Italian quilting, with the main exception that the design is marked in single lines which enclose the area to be raised or padded. The method of padding, however, is different and also applies to shadow quilting.

1 When the stitching is completed make an incision through the muslin into the area to be stuffed. Use a blunt needle to do this, or knitting needle if the area is large.

2 Remove the top skin of wadding and tease the wadding into small amounts which can easily be inserted through the incision. The amount of stuffing you use depends on the effect you desire.

3 When enough padding is inserted, close the opening with overcasting stitches before moving on to the next area.

Quilted pillow

This simple design for quilting can be modified and used to decorate various objects of home furnishings.

The directions are given for a pillow 16 inches × 12 inches, but the quilting can be adapted for a larger pillow by spacing out the motifs or for a small square pillow by omitting the small leaf shapes.

Fabric required

$\frac{3}{4}$ yd rayon fabric, or a not too shiny pure silk, or a dull satin, 36 in wide.

You will also need

$\frac{1}{2}$ yd thin cotton fabric, 36 in wide for backing the quilting.
$\frac{1}{2}$ yd synthetic wadding.
$1\frac{3}{4}$ yd cotton piping cord, No.2 size.
1 spool pure sewing silk to match the fabric.
1 spool mercerized sewing thread.
Tracing paper.
Thin white cardboard for the templates.
1 large fine-pointed darning needle.
Sewing needles (fine crewels or betweens) for quilting.
Pillow form to fit pillowcase.

Making the templates

1 Trace the heart and leaf motifs for the quilting onto the tracing paper.

2 Place the tracing onto the cardboard; pin or tape in position and cut around.

Working the quilting

1 Cut the quilting fabric to the size of the

finished pillow, plus $\frac{1}{2}$ inch all around for turnings.

Cut the wadding and the cotton backing fabric to the same size.

2 Baste the three layers together, sandwiching the wadding between the fabrics.
3 Mark the center lines of the fabric with basting diagonally from corner to corner.
4 Mount the fabric into the embroidery frame (see earlier).
5 Lay the mounted fabrics (in the frame) right side up on a folded blanket on a firm surface.
6 Position the heart template in the four positions as shown in the diagram. Holding the large needle at an angle, trace around the cardboard shape firmly enough to leave a sharp impression on the fabric. Take care not to cut the fabric with the needle point if your fabric is thin. Trace around the leaf shape at each end of the pillow. Place the smaller shape inside the heart and trace around.
7 Start to quilt the fabric, using the matching silk and working with a small even running stitch.
8 When the main motifs are completed, draw in the background diamond shapes using a ruler and large needle. Draw in the lines, working from each corner and keeping them $\frac{3}{4}$ inch apart. Quilt along the lines.
9 When the quilting is completed, remove it from the frame and fasten off all ends neatly.

Finishing the pillow case

1 From the surplus fabric, cut a piece the same size as the quilting for the back of the pillowcase and then cut bias strips 1½ inches wide for the piping casing. Make up the piping casing.

2 Pin the piping in position around the edge of the quilting and baste. Place the two sides of the pillowcase together with right sides facing. Baste and machine stitch using the mercerized sewing thread along the piping line. Leave one side of the pillowcase open and turn it right side out.

3 Insert a zipper into the open side and then insert the pillow form, or insert the form first and slip-stitch the sides of the opening together.

Traveling slippers and case
Fabric required
½ yd fabric for quilting, 36 in wide.
½ yd cotton fabric, 36 in wide, for the backing.
½ yd rayon lining fabric, 36 in wide.

You will also need
½ yd synthetic wadding.
One pair of foam rubber inner soles in required size.
Felt, to cover foam soles.
Vinyl fabric, to cover bottom of slippers.
Adhesive.
Quilting equipment as for pillowcase.

Working the quilting

1 Trace the shapes for the slipper fronts and case and baste the shapes onto the quilting fabric, allowing at least 1 inch

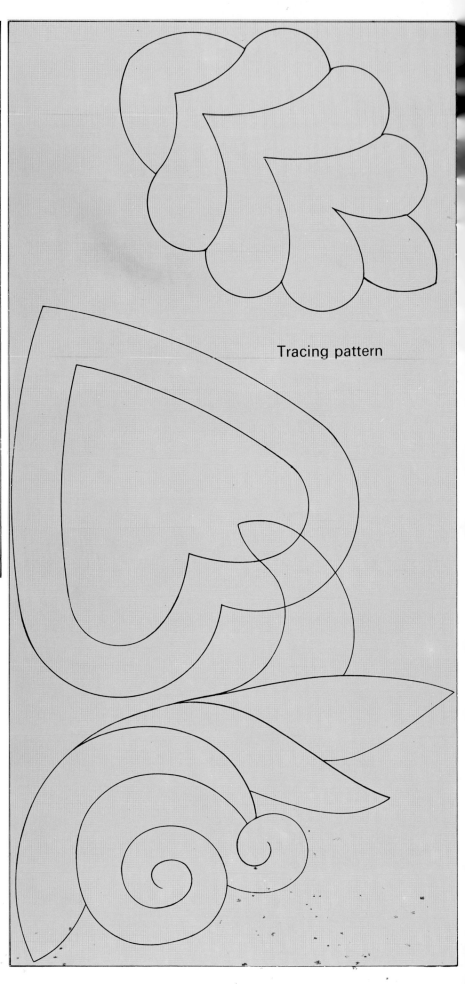

Tracing pattern

between each one.

2 Sandwich the wadding between the quilting fabric and cotton backing and baste the layers together. Mount them into an embroidery frame.

3 Mark the quilting shapes, using the leaf for the slippers and the scroll for the case. Work the quilting.

4 Mark the background diamond pattern, placing the lines $\frac{1}{2}$ inch apart.

Making the slippers

1 Cut around the basted shapes of the slippers, leaving 1 inch for turnings. Cut out linings for the slippers to the same size.

2 Cut bias strips and make piping about 5 inches long for each slipper. Baste in place along each top edge. Place the lining onto the slipper front with right sides

together and stitch close to the piping. Turn right side out and baste the lining and quilting together around the remaining edge.

3 Place the foam inner soles onto the felt and draw around, leaving $\frac{1}{2}$ inch turnings.

4 Clip into the turnings of the felt, place on to the foam inner soles and attach the turnings down on the underside.

5 Place the slipper fronts right side up onto the felt side of the soles, fold the turnings onto the underside and pin in position. Try on the slippers and adjust the size of the turnings if necessary. Secure in position with adhesive.

6 Cut two shapes of the soles from the vinyl fabric and stick in position on the underside to cover the raw edges of the quilting and felt.

Making the slipper case

1 Cut out the lining to the same size as the quilting.

2 Place the quilting and lining together with right sides facing and baste and machine stitch along the top curved edge, taking $\frac{1}{4}$ inch turnings. Clip into the angle and turn right side out.

3 Baste along the top seam so that no lining shows on the quilted side of the case. Press.

4 Fold the case in half so that the curved edges match and the quilted side is inside. Baste and machine stitch down the side and bottom edge, taking $\frac{1}{4}$ inch turnings. Make the edges neat by overcasting or zig-zag stitching. Turn the finished case right side out.

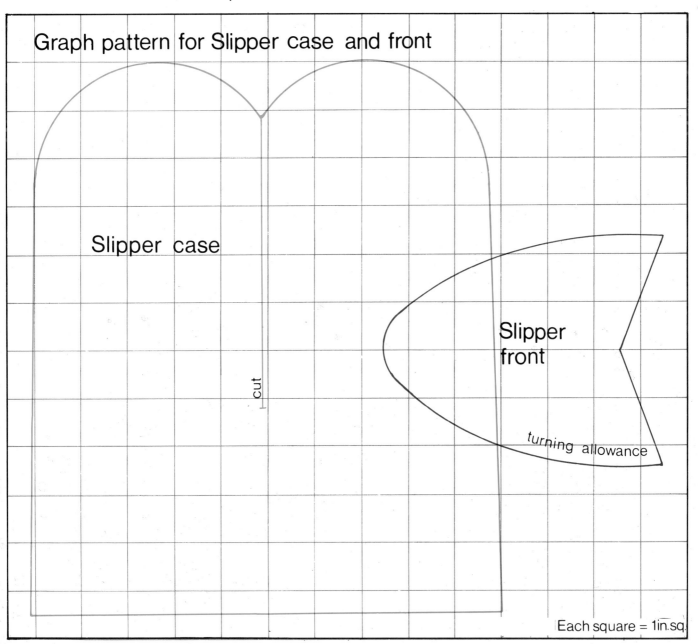

Graph pattern for Slipper case and front

Slipper case

Slipper front

cut

turning allowance

Each square = 1in.sq.

QUILTING BY MACHINE

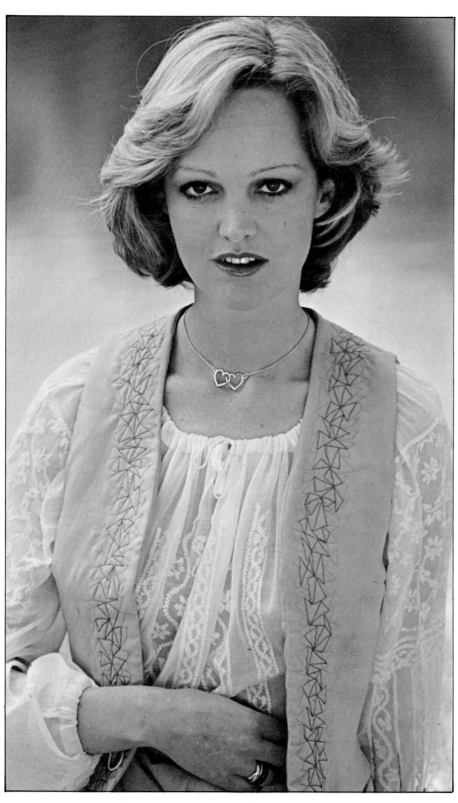

The cording foot and quilting

Most machines have a cording or braiding foot as an extra attachment. This foot guides a thick thread or cord under the needle. It can be straight stitched down the center, zigzagged or enclosed with satin stitch. This is an effective way of working solid shapes.

The shapes can be worked directly onto the article or on separate pieces of fabric which are then applied to give a more raised effect. The edges of the applied shapes can then be turned under and hemstitched so they are not visible; or the application may become part of the design and can be satin stitched for instance, or concealed with free embroidery. Whichever of these methods you choose the shapes should be worked from the outside toward the center so the shape does not become distorted.

The fabrics and threads

If the fabric is a fine one it will be necessary to back the shape with paper. Iron-on interfacing is excellent for dress embroidery providing the work does not have to drape.

A test sample should always be worked to make sure that the cord used is fine enough to be gripped firmly by the foot. A thicker cord might cause subsequent lines to be uneven and the groove on the underside of the foot, which allows for the passage of the thick thread, may catch on an adjacent line, thus dislodging the work. However, if you wish to use a thicker cord, this difficulty can be overcome by changing to the presser foot after the first round has been completed. To make stitching easier use soft yarns which flatten under the presser foot. Textured yarns may be used and generally look best if a matching thread is used to attach them. If a good match is not available, use transparent thread on top and the nearest color match in the bobbin.

Quilting can be used on its own or combined with areas of free embroidery or any other stitch effects already described. It can be worked in the usual way using the quilting foot and guide, and also in the hoop, making it possible to sew smaller and more intricate shapes. For the best effect the work should not be too tightly stretched in the hoop and only a limited amount of wadding can be used to allow it to fit into the hoop at all. For this reason it is better not to use a hoop with the inner ring bound. If, with the thickness of the work, the machine tends to skip stitches, use the darning foot and work with looser tensions. Quilting by this method could provide a decorative yoke and hem, or collar and cuffs for a dress.

Cotton, Dacron or thin foam make good fillers for quilting and the latter two have the advantage of being washable. Fine soft fabric should be used for the backing. Cotton lawn is excellent. Italian quilting is particularly attractive for garment embroidery. Two parallel lines of stitching are worked holding two fabrics together and thick yarn is inserted by hand from the back between the fabrics. The distance between the two lines is governed by the thickness of the yarn. If a fine fabric is used on top an attractive shadow effect can be achieved. An openweave fabric should be used for the backing to facilitate the wool insertion.

The stitches

Quilting may be worked in cable stitch in which case the design can be marked on tissue paper, basted to and worked from the wrong side, then torn away. Alternatively, the design may be drawn with tailor's chalk and worked from the right side by applying a fine embroidery thread with a zigzag stitch.

Work from the center of a design outward allowing plenty of extra fabric for the seam allowances. Do not trim the edges of cut-out pattern sections until the quilting has been completed.

The flower-shaped motif shown is worked freely in the hoop and the geometric motif is worked with the quilting foot. The design for the floral motif is marked on paper first and basted to the wrong side of the fabric. Cable stitch is worked from the wrong side, using a silky hand embroidery thread on the bobbin and sewing thread through the needle.

Pure silk thread is used for the straight stitching which is worked from the right side. The upper and lower tensions are balanced.

The quilted vest

A vest, such as the one illustrated, is ideal for quilting since the pattern can be worked on both front pieces and there are no buttonholes or buttons to work around. The pattern pieces are cut from 2oz. washable quilting, the dart shapes are cut out and the edges overcast together by hand. The lining is made up and the darts are worked on each remaining pattern piece. The quilting is then basted very firmly on the wrong side of those pieces. The embroidery is worked using the quilting foot. The thread and tensions used are the same as those for the motifs. When the embroidery is completed the vest is made up according to the instructions with the pattern. Hooks and eyes may be sewn at center-front if desired.

A GUIDE TO FABRICS AND THREADS

As more people are experimenting with the ever-increasing number of materials available now, the days when a particular type of embroidery was worked only on one specific type of fabric are past. This chart endeavors to give suggestions for both traditional methods and the more progressive ones and the fabrics and threads appropriate for each.

TYPE OF EMBROIDERY	TRADITIONAL USE		CONTEMPORARY USE	
	Fabrics	Threads	Fabrics	Threads
BASIC STITCHERY	Linen, cotton, rayon, stamped goods	Linen and silk	Any type of material from burlap to organdy	Wool, silk, cotton, nylon, chenille, cords, nylon string
QUILTING (Traditional Padding: carded sheep's wool, cotton wadding, or flannel) (Contemporary Padding: synthetic wadding)				
English	Fine silk, fine linen, dull satin, fine wool	Pure silk, fine linen and silk, silk	Shantung, satin, nylon, glazed cotton, poplin, viyella, fine wool	Pure silk
Italian	As above	As above	As above	As above
Trapunto	As above	As above	As above	As above
DRAWN (OR PULLED FABRIC)	Evenweave linen of various weights	Matching threads	Cotton, wool, linen, synthetic evenweave fabrics	Pearl cotton, Coton à broder, wool, and linen
Drawn thread	As above	As above	As above	As above
Blackwork	As above	As above	As above	As above
Hardanger	Evenweave cotton and linen	As above	As above plus tweed and flannel	Cotton, silk, and wool to contrast in weight and texture

TYPE OF EMBROIDERY	TRADITIONAL USE		CONTEMPORARY USE	
	Fabrics	**Threads**	**Fabrics**	**Threads**
Hedebo	As above	As above	As above	As above
Assisi	As above	As above	As above	As above
Cross-stitch	As above	As above	As above	As above
Needlepoint	Single and double canvas and linen	Crewel	Single and double canvas and linen	Crewel wools, tapestry wools, 6-strand floss, silk and crochet threads
SHADOW WORK	White organdy and muslin	Fine white	White and colored organdy, organza, chiffon, nylon	Pure silk, sewing silk for applied areas. Silk, wool, and 6-strand floss for embroidery
SMOCKING	Fine cotton, georgette, crêpe de chine, silk, fine wools and chiffon, fine linen	Silk, cotton, and linen (threads generally should be slightly heavier than the fabric)	Chiffon, cotton, wool, synthetics, some types of vinyl, corduroy, flannel and dress tweed	Crochet cotton, knitting wools, silk, buttonhole twist, linen embroidery
AYRSHIRE WORK AND EYELET EMBROIDERY (white work)	Fine linen, linen lawn, fine cotton, muslin, organdy (always white)	Matching fine cotton and linen, cotton floche and coton à broder	Cotton, organdy, linen lawn, Swiss cotton and muslin organza	Matching cotton, silk, and linen
CUTWORK				
Simple	White or natural linen	Matching linen, cotton, mercerized	Colored linen, strong cotton, dress tweed, home furnishing fabrics if firm woven	Matching linen and cotton
Renaissance embroidery	As above	As above	As above	As above
Richelieu embroidery	As above	As above	As above	Also fine crochet
Reticella embroidery	As above	As above	As above	As above
NEEDLEWEAVING	Loosely woven linen, linen crash, huckaback, and home furnishing fabrics	Threads should be slightly thicker than withdrawn thread	Burlap, canvas, heavy linens, linen scrim, dress tweeds	Any suitable to the weight and texture of the fabric being woven

A DICTIONARY OF STITCHES

An alphabet of free style embroidery stitches begins here and includes outline, flat, looped, chained, knotted, couching, filling and composite stitches. Diagrams and step-by-step instructions make the alphabet a useful source of reference material for both a beginner and the more experienced embroiderer.

Backstitch

Bring the thread through on the stitch line, then take a small backward stitch through the fabric. Bring the needle through again a little in front of the first stitch and take another stitch, inserting the needle at the point where it first came through.

Blanket stitch and buttonhole stitch

These stitches are worked in the same way – the difference being that in buttonhole stitch the stitches are close together. Bring the thread out on the lower line, insert the needle in position in the upper line, taking a straight downward stitch with the thread under the needle point. Pull up the stitch to form a loop and

repeat. This stitch may also be worked on evenweave fabric.

Bokhara couching

This stitch is useful and ornamental for filling in shapes of leaves and petals of flowers. It is worked in the same way as Rumanian stitch, but the small tying stitches are set at regular intervals over the laid thread to form pattern lines across the shape. The tying stitches should be pulled tight, leaving the laid thread slightly loose between.

Bullion stitch

Pick up a backstitch, the size of the bullion stitch required, bring the needle point out where it first emerged. Do not pull the needle right through the fabric. Wind the thread around the needle point as many times as required to equal the space of the backstitch. Hold the left thumb on the

coiled thread and pull the needle through; still holding the coiled thread, turn the needle back to where it was inserted (see arrow) and insert in the same place (A). Pull the thread through until the bullion stitch lies flat. Use a needle with a small eye to allow the thread to pass through the coils easily.

Buttonhole stitch bars and double buttonhole stitch bars

These bars are used in cut-work and Richelieu work. Make a row of running stitch between the double lines of the design as a padding for the buttonhole stitch. Where a single line bar occurs, take a thread across the space and back, securing with a small stitch and buttonhole stitch closely over the loose threads without picking up any of the fabric (A). Buttonhole stitch around the shape, keeping the looped edge of the stitch to the inside, then cut away the fabric from behind the bar and around the inside of the shape. Where a double line or a broad bar is required between shapes or for stems of flowers, when the fabric is to be cut away on each side, make a row of running stitch along one side, spacing the stitches slightly. Buttonhole stitch along the other side into the spaces left by the first row. The fabric is then cut away close to the buttonhole stitch, leaving a strong, broad bar (B).

Buttonhole insertion stitch

This insertion stitch consists of groups of four buttonhole stitches worked alternately on each piece of fabric to be joined. The upper row is worked as in ordinary buttonhole stitch. The diagram shows the method of working the groups on the lower row.

Buttonhole stitch and picot

Work as for ordinary buttonhole stitch until a picot is required, then hold the thread down with the left thumb and wind the needle three times around the thread (A). Still holding the thread securely, pull the working thread until the twisted threads are close to the buttonhole stitch, then make a buttonhole stitch into the last loop (B).

Cable stitch

This stitch is worked from left to right. Bring the thread through on the line of the design. Insert the needle a little to the right on the line and bring the needle out to the left midway between the length of the stitch, with the thread below the needle (Figure A). Work the next stitch in the same way but with the thread above the needle. Continue in this way, alternating the position of the thread. This stitch may also be worked on evenweave fabric (Figure B).

Cable chain stitch

Bring the thread through at A and hold it down with the left thumb. Pass the needle from right to left under the working thread, then twist the needle back over the working thread to the right and, still keeping the thread under the thumb, take a stitch of the required length. Pull the thread through over the loop.

Chain stitch

Bring the thread out at the top of the line and hold down with left thumb. Insert the needle where it last emerged and bring the point out a short distance away. Pull the thread through, keeping the working thread under the needle point.

Chained feather stitch

Working between two parallel lines, bring the thread through at A and make a slanting chain stitch, tying down the stitch at B. Take a second slanting chain stitch from the right at C, tying it down at D. The tying stitches will form a regular zig-zag pattern.

Checkered chain stitch

This stitch is worked in the same way as chain stitch, but with two contrasting threads in the needle at the same time. When making the loops, pass one color under the needle point and let the other color lie on top. Pull through both threads. Work the next loop with the other color under the needle point.

Chevron stitch

Bring the thread through on the lower line at the left side, insert the needle a little to the right on the same line and take a small stitch to the left, emerging halfway between the stitch being made. Next, insert the needle on the upper line a little to the right and take a small stitch to the left as at A. Insert the needle again on the same line a little to the right and take a small stitch to the left, emerging at the center as at B. Work in this way alternately on the upper and lower lines. This stitch may also be worked on evenweave fabric.

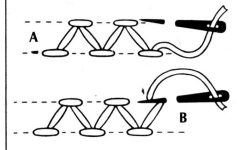

Closed buttonhole stitch

The stitches are made in pairs forming triangles. Bring the thread through at A, insert the needle at B and, with the thread under the needle, bring it through at C. Insert the needle again at B and bring it through at D. This stitch may also be worked on evenweave fabric.

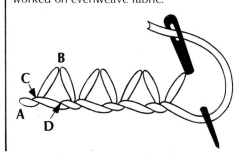

Closed feather stitch

This stitch is worked along two parallel lines. Bring the thread through at A and with the thread under the needle, take a stitch from B to C. Swing the thread over to the left and, with the thread under the needle, take a stitch from D to E. Repeat these two stitches.

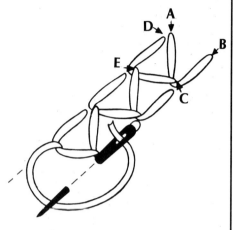

Coral stitch

Bring the thread out at the right side of the line, lay the thread along the line of the design and hold it down with the left thumb. Take a small stitch under the line and the thread and pull through, bringing the needle over the lower thread as in the diagram.

Couching

Lay a thread along the line of the design and, with another thread, tie it down at even intervals with a small stitch into the fabric. The tying stitch can be in a color which contrasts with the laid thread if desired.

Cretan stitch

Bring the needle through centrally at the left-hand side, taking a small stitch on the lower line, needle pointing inward and with the thread under the needle point, as shown at A. Take a stitch on the upper line and thread under the needle as shown at B. Continue in this way until shape is filled.

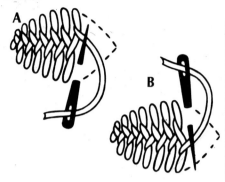

Cross stitch

Bring the needle through on the lower right line of the cross and insert at the top of the same line, taking a stitch through the fabric to the lower left line (Figure A).

Continue to the end of the row in this way. Complete the other half of the cross (Figure B). It is important that the upper half of each stitch lies in the same direction.

Double backstitch or closed herringbone stitch

This stitch is used for shadow work on fine, transparent fabric and can be worked on the right side of the fabric as at A – a small backstitch worked alternately on each side of the traced double lines (the dotted lines on the diagram show the formation of the thread on the wrong side of the fabric). The color of the thread appears delicately through the fabric. Figure B shows the stitch worked on the wrong side of the fabric as a closed herringbone stitch with no spaces left between the stitches. Both methods achieve the same result.

Daisy stitch or detached chain stitch

Work in the same way as chain stitch (A), but fasten each loop at the foot with a small stitch (B). Lazy daisy stitch may be

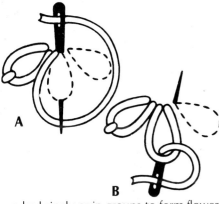

worked singly or in groups to form flower petals.

Double knot stitch

Bring the thread through at A. Take a small stitch across the line at B. Pass the needle downward under the surface stitch just made, without piercing the fabric, as at C. With the thread under the needle, pass

the needle again under the first stitch at D. Pull the thread through to form a knot. The knots should be spaced evenly and closely to obtain a beaded effect.

Eyelet holes

Figure A. Work a row of small running stitches around the circle. Pierce the center with a sharp pointed needle and fold back the ragged edge. Closely overcast the folded edge with running stitch. Trim away any ragged edges at the back. Figure B shows the appearance of the finished eyelet hole. Larger circles or longer eyelet holes may be cut across the center both ways and the cut ends folded back.

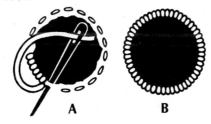

Feather stitch

Figure A. Bring the needle out at the top center, hold the thread down with the left thumb, insert the needle a little to the right on the same level and take a small stitch down to the center, keeping the thread under the needle point. Next, insert the needle a little to the left on the same level and take a stitch to center, keeping the thread under the needle point. Work these two movements alternately.

Figure B shows double feather stitch, in which two stitches are taken to the right and left alternately.

Fern stitch

This stitch consists of three straight stitches of equal length radiating from the same central point A. Bring the thread through at A and make a straight stitch to B. Bring the thread through again at A and make another straight stitch to C. Repeat once more to D and bring the thread through at E to begin the next three radiating stitches. The central stitch follows the line of the design. This stitch may also be worked on evenweave fabric.

Fishbone stitch

This stitch is useful for filling small shapes. Bring the thread through at A and make a small straight stitch along the center line of the shape. Bring the thread

153

through again at B and make a sloping stitch across the central line at the base of the first stitch. Bring the thread through at C and make a similar sloping stitch to overlap the previous stitch. Continue working alternately on each side until the shape is filled.

Flat stitch

Take a small stitch alternately on each side of the shape to be filled, with the point of the needle always emerging on the outside line of the shape. Two lines may be drawn down the center of the shape as a guide for the size of the stitch. The stitches should be close together and fold into one another.

Fly stitch

Bring the thread through at the top left, hold it down with the left thumb, insert the needle to the right on the same level, a little distance from where the thread first emerged and take a small stitch downward to the center with the thread below the needle. Pull through and insert the needle again below the stitch at the center (A) and bring it through in position for the next stitch. This stitch may be worked singly or in horizontal rows (A) or vertically (B).

French knots

Bring the thread out at the required position, hold it down with the left thumb and wind the thread twice around the needle as at A. Still holding the thread firmly, twist the needle back to the starting point and insert it close to where the thread first emerged (see arrow). Pull

the thread through to the back and secure for a single French knot or pass on to the position of the next stitch as at B.

Heavy chain stitch

Bring the thread through at A and make a small vertical stitch. Bring the thread through again at B and pass the needle under the vertical stitch, without piercing the fabric, and insert it again at B. Bring the thread through at C and again pass the needle under the vertical stitch and

insert it at C. The third and all following stitches are made in exactly the same way, except that the needle always passes under the two preceding loops.

Herringbone stitch

Bring the needle out on the lower line at the left side and insert on the upper line a little to the right, taking a small stitch to the left with the thread below the needle. Next, insert the needle on the lower line a little to the right and take a small stitch to the left with the thread above the needle. These two movements are worked throughout. For the best effect, the fabric lifted by the needle and the spaces between the stitches should be of equal size. This stitch can be laced with a matching or contrasting thread. Use a tapestry needle for lacing and do not pick up any of the fabric. Herringbone stitch may also be worked on evenweave fabric.

Interlaced band

This stitch is composed of two rows of backstitch with an interlacing. Work two parallel rows of backstitch (as shown at the top of the diagram) having the rows approximately $\frac{1}{2}$ to $\frac{3}{4}$ inch apart, with the stitches worked as on the diagram, i.e., the end of one stitch is directly in line with the center of the opposite stitch. Bring a matching or contrasting thread through at A and, following the diagram, interlace it through every stitch.

Interlacing stitch

The foundation of the border stitch is a double row of herringbone stitch worked in two steps, with the stitches intertwined in a certain way. The first row of herringbone stitch is shown in medium tone on the diagram. In working the rows of herringbone stitch for the interlacing, there is a slight change in the usual method. In the top stitch the needle is passed under the working thread in each case instead of over it, and attention should be paid to the alternate crossing of the threads when working the second row. Do not work this foundation tightly, as the interlacing thread tends to draw the stitches together. When the rows of herringbone stitch are worked, bring the thread for the surface interlacing through at A and follow the diagram closely. When the end of the row is reached, lace the thread around the last cross in the center and work back in a similar fashion along the lower half of the foundation. The last two crosses on the diagram have been left unlaced so that the construction of the herringbone stitch may be seen clearly.

Jacobean couching or trellis

This stitch makes an attractive filling stitch for the centers of flowers or shapes where an open effect is required. It consists of long evenly spaced stitches (laid threads) taken across the space horizontally and vertically (A) or diagonally (B). The crossed threads are then tied down at all intersecting points. The tying or couching stitch can be a small slanting stitch or cross-stitch.

Knot stitch edging or Antwerp edging

Bring the thread through from the back of the fabric and work a single buttonhole stitch. Pass the needle behind the loop of the stitch and over the working thread as shown in the diagram. Space the stitches about $\frac{1}{4}$ inch apart. This edging is very useful for handkerchiefs or lingerie. Several rows, using a different color for each row, make a lacy edging. The stitches of the second and following rows are worked over the loops between the stitches of the previous row.

Knotted buttonhole stitch

Make a loop from right to left over the left thumb. Insert the needle, point upward, under the loop as at A. Slip the loop onto the needle and, with the loop still around the needle, take a stitch into the fabric as at B. Before drawing the needle through, tighten the loop around the head of the needle by pulling the working thread.

Knotted buttonhole filling stitch

Make an outline of backstitch or close running stitches, then work the detached filling as shown in the diagram. The link with the edging stitches is especially large for clarity.

Knotted cable chain stitch

This stitch is worked from right to left. Bring the thread through at A and place it along the line of the design; then, with the thread under the needle, take a stitch at B, which is a coral knot. Then pass the needle under the stitch between A and B without piercing the fabric, as shown at C. With the thread under the needle, take a slanting stitch across the line at D, close to the coral knot. Pull the thread through to form a chain stitch.

Knotted insertion stitch

This stitch is similar to knot stitch (or Antwerp stitch) edging, except that the stitches are made alternately on each piece of fabric to be joined. A small buttonhole stitch is worked into the edge of the fabric and a second stitch worked over the loops as shown in the figure.

Laced running stitch

Running stitch can be laced with a contrasting color to form a decorative border. Use a tapestry needle for lacing and do not pick up any of the fabric.

Ladder stitch

This stitch may be used to fill shapes of varying widths, but it is shown worked between parallel lines. Bring the thread through at A, insert the needle at B and bring it out at C. Insert the needle again at D and bring out at E. Pass the needle under the first stitch at F and through the double stitch at G. Continue in this way, the needle passing under two stitches at each side to form the braided edge.

Leaf stitch

Bring the thread through at A and make a sloping stitch to B. Bring the thread through at C and make a sloping stitch to D. Bring the thread through at E, then continue working alternate stitches on each side in this way until the shape is lightly filled. This stitch is generally finished with an outline worked in stem stitch or chain stitch.

Long and short stitch

This form of satin stitch is so named because all the stitches are of varying lengths. It is often used to fill a shape which is too large or too irregular to be covered by ordinary satin stitch. It is also used to achieve a shaded effect. In the first row the stitches are alternately long and short and closely follow the outline of the shape. The stitches in the following rows are worked to achieve a smooth appearance. The figure shows how a shaded effect may be obtained.

Loop stitch

This stitch is worked from right to left. Bring the thread through at A and insert the needle at B. Bring it through again at C immediately below B. With the thread to the left and under the needle, pass the needle under the first stitch without piercing the fabric.

Maltese cross

This decorative motif is worked in a similar way to interlacing stitch. The intertwining of the herringbone stitch must be worked accurately, otherwise the interlacing cannot be achieved. Bring the thread through at A and take a stitch from B to C. Carry the thread from C to D and take a stitch from D to E. Continue in this way following Figure 1 until the foundation is complete. Figure 2 shows the method of interlacing, which begins at F. Figure 3 shows the completed motif.

Open chain stitch

This stitch is shown worked on two parallel lines, but it may be used for shapes which vary in width. Bring the thread through at A and, holding the thread

down with the left thumb, insert the needle at B. Bring the needle through at C, the required depth of the stitch. Leave the loop thus formed slightly loose. Insert the needle at D and, with the thread under the needle point, bring it through in readiness for the next stitch. Secure the last loop with a small stitch at each side.

Open Cretan stitch

Bring the thread through at A and, with the thread above the needle, insert the needle at B and bring it through at C. With the thread below the needle, insert the needle at D and bring it through at E. All stitches lie at right angles to the guide lines as shown in the diagram and are spaced at regular intervals. This is a useful stitch for borders.

Open fishbone stitch

Bring the thread through at A and make a sloping stitch to B. Bring the thread through again at C and make another sloping stitch to D. Bring the thread through at E, continue in this way until the shape is filled.

Overcast stitch (or trailing)

Bring the laid threads through at A and hold with the left thumb, then bring through the working thread at A and work small satin stitches closely over the laid threads, following the line of the design.

The laid threads are taken through to the back of the fabric to finish. This stitch resembles a fine cord and is useful for embroidering delicate stems and outlines.

Pekinese stitch

Work backstitch in the usual way, then interlace with a thread to tone or a thread of a different color. The stitch is shown open in the diagram but the loops should be pulled slightly tighter when working.

Portuguese border stitch

Work the required number of foundation bars, which are evenly spaced horizontal straight stitches. Bring the thread through at A, with the working thread to the left of the needle. Carry it over and under the first two bars and under the second bar only, without piercing the fabric. The thread is now in position at B to start the second pair of stitches. Continue working in the same way to the top of the row. Bring a new thread through at C and proceed in exactly the same way, but with the working thread to the right of the needle. Do not pull the surface stitches tightly.

Portuguese stem stitch

Figure A, begin as for ordinary stem stitch. Figure B, pull the thread through and pass the needle under the stitch just made, without entering the fabric. Figure C, pass the needle under the same stitch below the first coil. Figure D, make another stem stitch. Figure E, pass the needle twice under the stitch just made and under the previous stitch. Figure F, a section showing the formation of the stitch.

Punch stitch

This stitch can be used as a filling stitch in free embroidery – that is, over a tracing of squares or spots. A punch needle is used for the traced design to make the holes. The stitches are pulled firmly. Bring the thread through and take a stitch directly above, bringing the needle out where the thread first emerged (A). Insert the needle into the same hole above and bring out the same distance to the left on the lower line (B). Work along the row in this way, two stitches into the same place in each case (C). Turn the work upside down for each following row and continue in the same way until all vertical rows are complete (D). Turn the work sideways and repeat the process to complete the squares (E).

Raised chain band

Work the required number of foundation bars, which are fairly closely spaced horizontal straight stitches. Bring the thread through at A, then pass the needle upward under the center of the first bar and to the left of A. With the thread under the needle, pass the needle downward to the right of A and pull up the chain loop thus formed.

Rosette chain stitch

Bring the thread through at the right end of the upper line, pass the thread across to the left side and hold down with the left thumb. Insert the needle into the upper line a short distance from where the thread emerged and bring it out just above the lower line, passing the thread under the needle point (A). Draw the needle through and then pass the needle under the top thread (B) without picking up any of the fabric. This stitch can be used for small flowers if worked around in a circle or for borders when worked straight.

Rumanian couching

This form of couching is useful for filling in large spaces in which a flat, indefinite background is required. Bring the thread through on the left, carry the thread across the space to be filled and take a small stitch on the right with the thread above the needle (A). Take small stitches along the line at intervals, as in B and C, to the end of the laid thread, emerging in position for the next stitch (D).

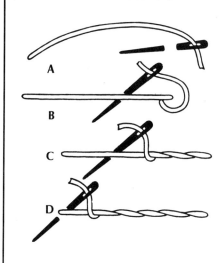

Rumanian stitch

Figure A, bring the thread through at the top left of the shape, carry the thread across and take a stitch on the right side of the shape with the thread below the needle. Figure B, take a stitch at the left side, thread above the needle. These two movements are worked until the shape is filled. Keep the stitches close together. The size of the center crossing stitch can be varied to make a longer diagonal stitch or a small straight stitch.

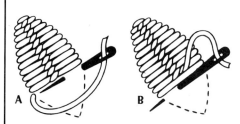

Running stitch

Pass the needle over and under the fabric, making the upper stitches of equal length. The under stitches should also be of equal length, but half the size or less of the upper stitches.

Satin stitch

Work straight stitches worked closely together across the shape, as shown in the diagram. If desired, running stitch or chain stitch may be worked first to form a padding underneath, giving a raised effect. Care must be taken to keep a good edge. Do not make the stitches too long, as this makes them liable to be pulled out of position. To keep a good edge, outline the shape first in chain or split stitch.

Scroll stitch

This stitch is worked from left to right. The working thread is looped to the right then back to the left on the fabric. Inside this loop the needle takes a small slanting stitch to the left under the line of the design, with the thread of the loop under the needle point. The thread is then pulled through. The stitches should be evenly spaced. This stitch forms an attractive border.

Seeding

This simple filling stitch is composed of small straight stitches of equal length placed at random over the surface, as shown in the figure.

Sheaf stitch

This is an attractive filling stitch consisting of three vertical satin stitches tied across the center with two horizontal overcasting stitches. The overcasting stitches are worked around the satin stitches; the needle only enters the fabric to pass on to the next sheaf. The sheaves may be worked in alternate rows as shown, or in close horizontal rows directly below each other.

Spanish knotted feather stitch

Bring the thread through and hold down to the left with the left thumb. Take a slanting stitch to the left through the fabric under the laid thread and pull through with the needle point over the working thread as shown at A. Pass the thread over to the right and back to the left to form a loop and hold down, then take a slanting stitch to the right under the laid thread and pull through with the needle over the working thread B. Take a stitch in the same way to the left as at C. Repeat B and C to the end of the line, then fasten off with a small stitch as shown at D.

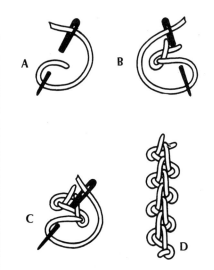

Spider's web filling, woven

Begin with a fly stitch to the center of the circle as shown in A. Then work two straight stitches, one on each side of the fly stitch tail, into the center of the circle. This divides the circle into five equal sections and the "spokes" form the foundation of the web. Weave over and under the "spokes" until the circle is filled as at B. In drawn thread embroidery the "spokes" are not completely covered by the weaving; only half the circle is filled, which gives the filling an open, lacy appearance.

Split stitch

Bring the thread through at A and make a small stitch over the line of the design, piercing the working thread with the needle as shown in the figure. Split stitch may be used as a filling where a fine flat surface is required.

Stem stitch

Work from left to right, taking regular, slightly slanting stitches along the line of the design. The thread always emerges on the left side of the previous stitch. This stitch is used for flower stems, outlines, etc. It can also be used as a filling, where rows of stem stitch are worked closely together within a shape until it is filled completely.

Straight stitch or single satin stitch

This is shown as single spaced stitches worked either in a regular or irregular manner. Sometimes the stitches are of varying size. The stitches should be neither too long nor too loose. This stitch may also be worked on evenweave fabric.

Striped woven band

Work the required number of foundation bars which are evenly spaced horizontal straight stitches. Thread two needles with contrasting threads and bring them through the fabric to lie side by side at A, the light thread on the left side. Pass the light thread under the first straight stitch and leave it lying. Take the dark thread over the first straight stitch and under the second straight stitch and also under the light thread. Leave the dark thread lying and pass the light thread over the second straight stitch, under the third straight stitch and also under the dark thread. Continue to the end of the border. Begin each following row from the top. By altering the sequence of the contrasting threads, various patterns may be achieved.

Twisted chain stitch

Begin as for ordinary chain stitch, but instead of inserting the needle into the place from where it emerged, insert it close to the last loop and take a small slanting stitch, coming out on the line of the design. Pull the thread through. The loops of this stitch should be worked closely together to give the correct effect.

Twisted insertion stitch

A small stitch is taken alternately on each piece of fabric to be joined. The needle always enters the fabric from beneath and is twisted once around the thread before entering the fabric for the opposite stitch.

Up and down buttonhole stitch

Figure A. Begin as for ordinary buttonhole stitch and pull thread through. Figure B. Insert the needle on the bottom line and take a straight upward stitch with the thread under the needle point. Pull the thread through first in an upward move-ment, then downward to continue. This stitch may also be worked on evenweave fabric.

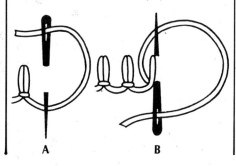

A   B

Vandyke stitch

Bring the thread through at A. Take a small horizontal stitch at B and insert the needle at C. Bring the thread through at D. Without piercing the fabric, pass the needle under the crossed threads at B and insert at E. Do not pull the stitches too tightly, otherwise the regularity of the center braid will be lost.

Wheatear stitch

Work two straight stitches at A and B. Bring the thread through below these stitches at C and pass the needle under the two straight stitches without entering the fabric. Insert the needle at C and bring it through at D.

Zigzag cable chain stitch

This stitch is a variation of ordinary cable chain stitch, each stitch being taken at a right angle to the previous stitch. Pull the twisted thread firmly around the needle before drawing the needle through the fabric.